C-3544 CAREER EXAMINATION SERIES

This is your
PASSBOOK for...

Motor Vehicle Supervisor

Test Preparation Study Guide
Questions & Answers

NLC®

NATIONAL LEARNING CORPORATION®

National Learning Corporation

212 Michael Drive, Syosset, NY 11791
(516) 921-8888 • www.passbooks.com
E-mail: info@passbooks.com

PUBLISHED IN THE UNITED STATES OF AMERICA

PASSBOOK® SERIES

THE *PASSBOOK® SERIES* has been created to prepare applicants and candidates for the ultimate academic battlefield – the examination room.

At some time in our lives, each and every one of us may be required to take an examination – for validation, matriculation, admission, qualification, registration, certification, or licensure.

Based on the assumption that every applicant or candidate has met the basic formal educational standards, has taken the required number of courses, and read the necessary texts, the *PASSBOOK® SERIES* furnishes the one special preparation which may assure passing with confidence, instead of failing with insecurity. Examination questions – together with answers – are furnished as the basic vehicle for study so that the mysteries of the examination and its compounding difficulties may be eliminated or diminished by a sure method.

This book is meant to help you pass your examination provided that you qualify and are serious in your objective.

The entire field is reviewed through the huge store of content information which is succinctly presented through a provocative and challenging approach – the question-and-answer method.

A climate of success is established by furnishing the correct answers at the end of each test.

You soon learn to recognize types of questions, forms of questions, and patterns of questioning. You may even begin to anticipate expected outcomes.

You perceive that many questions are repeated or adapted so that you can gain acute insights, which may enable you to score many sure points.

You learn how to confront new questions, or types of questions, and to attack them confidently and work out the correct answers.

You note objectives and emphases, and recognize pitfalls and dangers, so that you may make positive educational adjustments.

Moreover, you are kept fully informed in relation to new concepts, methods, practices, and directions in the field.

You discover that you are actually taking the examination all the time: you are preparing for the examination by "taking" an examination, not by reading extraneous and/or supererogatory textbooks.

In short, this PASSBOOK®, used directedly, should be an important factor in helping you to pass your test.

MOTOR VEHICLE SUPERVISOR

DUTIES AND RESPONSIBILITIES

Under general supervision, supervises automotive servicing operations of a departmental garage, and/or is responsible for the dispatching of the personnel, motor vehicles and equipment assigned to a large garage; performs related work.

EXAMPLES OF TYPICAL TASKS

Schedules subordinate personnel for the servicing, minor repairing, and storage of automotive vehicles. Makes daily inspection of garage activities and facilities to ensure compliance with established standards and practices. Investigates complaints on automotive servicing and operations. Receives reports of the condition of motor vehicles and equipment repaired or needing repairs, directing the performance of minor repairs, or, as to major repairs, referring their performance to appropriate repair sections. Reviews the utilization of motor vehicles and equipment by the different divisions of a department to determine efficient schedules of storage and servicing, and economical employment of facilities and garage personnel. Prepares and enforces routines of periodic oiling, lubrication, and washing of vehicles, their tire servicing, and the dispensing of gasoline as authorized for vehicular uses. Deals with vendors to obtain servicing, repairs, equipment, and materials. Initiates requisitions for needed. supplies and automotive servicing equipment. Supervises the maintenance of the garage and adjacent servicing. premises in a clean and safe condition, with attention to the provision and operating condition of required fire safeguards. Selects and dispatches suitable motor equipment to various jobs. Prepares trip instructions and designates the routes to be followed. Investigates accidents in which assigned vehicles have been involved. Prepares and reviews accident reports. Keeps attendance records, and keeps records on the daily consumption of gasoline and oil and on the departure and arrival of motor vehicles. Checks condition of incoming and outgoing motor vehicles. Instructs employees in the operation of specialized motor equipment, such as wreckers and heavy trucks. Occasionally drives motor vehicles. May do automotive servicing in emergencies.

TESTS

The written test will be of the multiple-choice type and may include questions on supervision of employees; maintenance of facilities; automotive maintenance; vehicle storage, servicing, routing, and dispatching; garage operations; maintenance of records; preparation and review of reports; and other related areas. .

HOW TO TAKE A TEST

I. YOU MUST PASS AN EXAMINATION

A. WHAT EVERY CANDIDATE SHOULD KNOW

Examination applicants often ask us for help in preparing for the written test. What can I study in advance? What kinds of questions will be asked? How will the test be given? How will the papers be graded?

As an applicant for a civil service examination, you may be wondering about some of these things. Our purpose here is to suggest effective methods of advance study and to describe civil service examinations.

Your chances for success on this examination can be increased if you know how to prepare. Those "pre-examination jitters" can be reduced if you know what to expect. You can even experience an adventure in good citizenship if you know why civil service exams are given.

B. WHY ARE CIVIL SERVICE EXAMINATIONS GIVEN?

Civil service examinations are important to you in two ways. As a citizen, you want public jobs filled by employees who know how to do their work. As a job seeker, you want a fair chance to compete for that job on an equal footing with other candidates. The best-known means of accomplishing this two-fold goal is the competitive examination.

Exams are widely publicized throughout the nation. They may be administered for jobs in federal, state, city, municipal, town or village governments or agencies.

Any citizen may apply, with some limitations, such as the age or residence of applicants. Your experience and education may be reviewed to see whether you meet the requirements for the particular examination. When these requirements exist, they are reasonable and applied consistently to all applicants. Thus, a competitive examination may cause you some uneasiness now, but it is your privilege and safeguard.

C. HOW ARE CIVIL SERVICE EXAMS DEVELOPED?

Examinations are carefully written by trained technicians who are specialists in the field known as "psychological measurement," in consultation with recognized authorities in the field of work that the test will cover. These experts recommend the subject matter areas or skills to be tested; only those knowledges or skills important to your success on the job are included. The most reliable books and source materials available are used as references. Together, the experts and technicians judge the difficulty level of the questions.

Test technicians know how to phrase questions so that the problem is clearly stated. Their ethics do not permit "trick" or "catch" questions. Questions may have been tried out on sample groups, or subjected to statistical analysis, to determine their usefulness.

Written tests are often used in combination with performance tests, ratings of training and experience, and oral interviews. All of these measures combine to form the best-known means of finding the right person for the right job.

II. HOW TO PASS THE WRITTEN TEST

A. NATURE OF THE EXAMINATION

To prepare intelligently for civil service examinations, you should know how they differ from school examinations you have taken. In school you were assigned certain definite pages to read or subjects to cover. The examination questions were quite detailed and usually emphasized memory. Civil service exams, on the other hand, try to discover your present ability to perform the duties of a position, plus your potentiality to learn these duties. In other words, a civil service exam attempts to predict how successful you will be. Questions cover such a broad area that they cannot be as minute and detailed as school exam questions.

In the public service similar kinds of work, or positions, are grouped together in one "class." This process is known as *position-classification*. All the positions in a class are paid according to the salary range for that class. One class title covers all of these positions, and they are all tested by the same examination.

B. FOUR BASIC STEPS

1) Study the announcement

How, then, can you know what subjects to study? Our best answer is: "Learn as much as possible about the class of positions for which you've applied." The exam will test the knowledge, skills and abilities needed to do the work.

Your most valuable source of information about the position you want is the official exam announcement. This announcement lists the training and experience qualifications. Check these standards and apply only if you come reasonably close to meeting them.

The brief description of the position in the examination announcement offers some clues to the subjects which will be tested. Think about the job itself. Review the duties in your mind. Can you perform them, or are there some in which you are rusty? Fill in the blank spots in your preparation.

Many jurisdictions preview the written test in the exam announcement by including a section called "Knowledge and Abilities Required," "Scope of the Examination," or some similar heading. Here you will find out specifically what fields will be tested.

2) Review your own background

Once you learn in general what the position is all about, and what you need to know to do the work, ask yourself which subjects you already know fairly well and which need improvement. You may wonder whether to concentrate on improving your strong areas or on building some background in your fields of weakness. When the announcement has specified "some knowledge" or "considerable knowledge," or has used adjectives like "beginning principles of..." or "advanced ... methods," you can get a clue as to the number and difficulty of questions to be asked in any given field. More questions, and hence broader coverage, would be included for those subjects which are more important in the work. Now weigh your strengths and weaknesses against the job requirements and prepare accordingly.

3) Determine the level of the position

Another way to tell how intensively you should prepare is to understand the level of the job for which you are applying. Is it the entering level? In other words, is this the position in which beginners in a field of work are hired? Or is it an intermediate or advanced level? Sometimes this is indicated by such words as "Junior" or "Senior" in the class title. Other jurisdictions use Roman numerals to designate the level – Clerk I, Clerk II, for example. The word "Supervisor" sometimes appears in the title. If the level is not indicated by the title, check the description of duties. Will you be working under very close supervision, or will you have responsibility for independent decisions in this work?

4) Choose appropriate study materials

Now that you know the subjects to be examined and the relative amount of each subject to be covered, you can choose suitable study materials. For beginning level jobs, or even advanced ones, if you have a pronounced weakness in some aspect of your training, read a modern, standard textbook in that field. Be sure it is up to date and has general coverage. Such books are normally available at your library, and the librarian will be glad to help you locate one. For entry-level positions, questions of appropriate difficulty are chosen – neither highly advanced questions, nor those too simple. Such questions require careful thought but not advanced training.

If the position for which you are applying is technical or advanced, you will read more advanced, specialized material. If you are already familiar with the basic principles of your field, elementary textbooks would waste your time. Concentrate on advanced textbooks and technical periodicals. Think through the concepts and review difficult problems in your field.

These are all general sources. You can get more ideas on your own initiative, following these leads. For example, training manuals and publications of the government agency which employs workers in your field can be useful, particularly for technical and professional positions. A letter or visit to the government department involved may result in more specific study suggestions, and certainly will provide you with a more definite idea of the exact nature of the position you are seeking.

III. KINDS OF TESTS

Tests are used for purposes other than measuring knowledge and ability to perform specified duties. For some positions, it is equally important to test ability to make adjustments to new situations or to profit from training. In others, basic mental abilities not dependent on information are essential. Questions which test these things may not appear as pertinent to the duties of the position as those which test for knowledge and information. Yet they are often highly important parts of a fair examination. For very general questions, it is almost impossible to help you direct your study efforts. What we can do is to point out some of the more common of these general abilities needed in public service positions and describe some typical questions.

1) General information

Broad, general information has been found useful for predicting job success in some kinds of work. This is tested in a variety of ways, from vocabulary lists to questions about current events. Basic background in some field of work, such as sociology or economics, may be sampled in a group of questions. Often these are principles which have become familiar to most persons through exposure rather than through formal training. It is difficult to advise you how to study for these questions; being alert to the world around you is our best suggestion.

2) Verbal ability

An example of an ability needed in many positions is verbal or language ability. Verbal ability is, in brief, the ability to use and understand words. Vocabulary and grammar tests are typical measures of this ability. Reading comprehension or paragraph interpretation questions are common in many kinds of civil service tests. You are given a paragraph of written material and asked to find its central meaning.

3) Numerical ability

Number skills can be tested by the familiar arithmetic problem, by checking paired lists of numbers to see which are alike and which are different, or by interpreting charts and graphs. In the latter test, a graph may be printed in the test booklet which you are asked to use as the basis for answering questions.

4) Observation

A popular test for law-enforcement positions is the observation test. A picture is shown to you for several minutes, then taken away. Questions about the picture test your ability to observe both details and larger elements.

5) Following directions

In many positions in the public service, the employee must be able to carry out written instructions dependably and accurately. You may be given a chart with several columns, each column listing a variety of information. The questions require you to carry out directions involving the information given in the chart.

6) Skills and aptitudes

Performance tests effectively measure some manual skills and aptitudes. When the skill is one in which you are trained, such as typing or shorthand, you can practice. These tests are often very much like those given in business school or high school courses. For many of the other skills and aptitudes, however, no short-time preparation can be made. Skills and abilities natural to you or that you have developed throughout your lifetime are being tested.

Many of the general questions just described provide all the data needed to answer the questions and ask you to use your reasoning ability to find the answers. Your best preparation for these tests, as well as for tests of facts and ideas, is to be at your physical and mental best. You, no doubt, have your own methods of getting into an exam-taking mood and keeping "in shape." The next section lists some ideas on this subject.

IV. KINDS OF QUESTIONS

Only rarely is the "essay" question, which you answer in narrative form, used in civil service tests. Civil service tests are usually of the short-answer type. Full instructions for answering these questions will be given to you at the examination. But in case this is your first experience with short-answer questions and separate answer sheets, here is what you need to know:

1) Multiple-choice Questions

Most popular of the short-answer questions is the "multiple choice" or "best answer" question. It can be used, for example, to test for factual knowledge, ability to solve problems or judgment in meeting situations found at work.

A multiple-choice question is normally one of three types—

- It can begin with an incomplete statement followed by several possible endings. You are to find the one ending which *best* completes the statement, although some of the others may not be entirely wrong.
- It can also be a complete statement in the form of a question which is answered by choosing one of the statements listed.

- It can be in the form of a problem – again you select the best answer.

Here is an example of a multiple-choice question with a discussion which should give you some clues as to the method for choosing the right answer:

When an employee has a complaint about his assignment, the action which will *best* help him overcome his difficulty is to
  A. discuss his difficulty with his coworkers
  B. take the problem to the head of the organization
  C. take the problem to the person who gave him the assignment
  D. say nothing to anyone about his complaint

In answering this question, you should study each of the choices to find which is best. Consider choice "A" – Certainly an employee may discuss his complaint with fellow employees, but no change or improvement can result, and the complaint remains unresolved. Choice "B" is a poor choice since the head of the organization probably does not know what assignment you have been given, and taking your problem to him is known as "going over the head" of the supervisor. The supervisor, or person who made the assignment, is the person who can clarify it or correct any injustice. Choice "C" is, therefore, correct. To say nothing, as in choice "D," is unwise. Supervisors have and interest in knowing the problems employees are facing, and the employee is seeking a solution to his problem.

2) True/False Questions

The "true/false" or "right/wrong" form of question is sometimes used. Here a complete statement is given. Your job is to decide whether the statement is right or wrong.

SAMPLE: A roaming cell-phone call to a nearby city costs less than a non-roaming call to a distant city.

This statement is wrong, or false, since roaming calls are more expensive.

This is not a complete list of all possible question forms, although most of the others are variations of these common types. You will always get complete directions for answering questions. Be sure you understand *how* to mark your answers – ask questions until you do.

V. RECORDING YOUR ANSWERS

Computer terminals are used more and more today for many different kinds of exams.

For an examination with very few applicants, you may be told to record your answers in the test booklet itself. Separate answer sheets are much more common. If this separate answer sheet is to be scored by machine – and this is often the case – it is highly important that you mark your answers correctly in order to get credit.

An electronic scoring machine is often used in civil service offices because of the speed with which papers can be scored. Machine-scored answer sheets must be marked with a pencil, which will be given to you. This pencil has a high graphite content which responds to the electronic scoring machine. As a matter of fact, stray dots may register as answers, so do not let your pencil rest on the answer sheet while you are pondering the correct answer. Also, if your pencil lead breaks or is otherwise defective, ask for another.

Since the answer sheet will be dropped in a slot in the scoring machine, be careful not to bend the corners or get the paper crumpled.

The answer sheet normally has five vertical columns of numbers, with 30 numbers to a column. These numbers correspond to the question numbers in your test booklet. After each number, going across the page are four or five pairs of dotted lines. These short dotted lines have small letters or numbers above them. The first two pairs may also have a "T" or "F" above the letters. This indicates that the first two pairs only are to be used if the questions are of the true-false type. If the questions are multiple choice, disregard the "T" and "F" and pay attention only to the small letters or numbers.

Answer your questions in the manner of the sample that follows:

32. The largest city in the United States is
    A. Washington, D.C.
    B. New York City
    C. Chicago
    D. Detroit
    E. San Francisco

1) Choose the answer you think is best. (New York City is the largest, so "B" is correct.)
2) Find the row of dotted lines numbered the same as the question you are answering. (Find row number 32)
3) Find the pair of dotted lines corresponding to the answer. (Find the pair of lines under the mark "B.")
4) Make a solid black mark between the dotted lines.

VI. BEFORE THE TEST

Common sense will help you find procedures to follow to get ready for an examination. Too many of us, however, overlook these sensible measures. Indeed, nervousness and fatigue have been found to be the most serious reasons why applicants fail to do their best on civil service tests. Here is a list of reminders:

- Begin your preparation early – Don't wait until the last minute to go scurrying around for books and materials or to find out what the position is all about.
- Prepare continuously – An hour a night for a week is better than an all-night cram session. This has been definitely established. What is more, a night a week for a month will return better dividends than crowding your study into a shorter period of time.
- Locate the place of the exam – You have been sent a notice telling you when and where to report for the examination. If the location is in a different town or otherwise unfamiliar to you, it would be well to inquire the best route and learn something about the building.
- Relax the night before the test – Allow your mind to rest. Do not study at all that night. Plan some mild recreation or diversion; then go to bed early and get a good night's sleep.
- Get up early enough to make a leisurely trip to the place for the test – This way unforeseen events, traffic snarls, unfamiliar buildings, etc. will not upset you.
- Dress comfortably – A written test is not a fashion show. You will be known by number and not by name, so wear something comfortable.

- Leave excess paraphernalia at home – Shopping bags and odd bundles will get in your way. You need bring only the items mentioned in the official notice you received; usually everything you need is provided. Do not bring reference books to the exam. They will only confuse those last minutes and be taken away from you when in the test room.
- Arrive somewhat ahead of time – If because of transportation schedules you must get there very early, bring a newspaper or magazine to take your mind off yourself while waiting.
- Locate the examination room – When you have found the proper room, you will be directed to the seat or part of the room where you will sit. Sometimes you are given a sheet of instructions to read while you are waiting. Do not fill out any forms until you are told to do so; just read them and be prepared.
- Relax and prepare to listen to the instructions
- If you have any physical problem that may keep you from doing your best, be sure to tell the test administrator. If you are sick or in poor health, you really cannot do your best on the exam. You can come back and take the test some other time.

VII. AT THE TEST

The day of the test is here and you have the test booklet in your hand. The temptation to get going is very strong. Caution! There is more to success than knowing the right answers. You must know how to identify your papers and understand variations in the type of short-answer question used in this particular examination. Follow these suggestions for maximum results from your efforts:

1) Cooperate with the monitor

The test administrator has a duty to create a situation in which you can be as much at ease as possible. He will give instructions, tell you when to begin, check to see that you are marking your answer sheet correctly, and so on. He is not there to guard you, although he will see that your competitors do not take unfair advantage. He wants to help you do your best.

2) Listen to all instructions

Don't jump the gun! Wait until you understand all directions. In most civil service tests you get more time than you need to answer the questions. So don't be in a hurry. Read each word of instructions until you clearly understand the meaning. Study the examples, listen to all announcements and follow directions. Ask questions if you do not understand what to do.

3) Identify your papers

Civil service exams are usually identified by number only. You will be assigned a number; you must not put your name on your test papers. Be sure to copy your number correctly. Since more than one exam may be given, copy your exact examination title.

4) Plan your time

Unless you are told that a test is a "speed" or "rate of work" test, speed itself is usually not important. Time enough to answer all the questions will be provided, but this does not mean that you have all day. An overall time limit has been set. Divide the total time (in minutes) by the number of questions to determine the approximate time you have for each question.

5) Do not linger over difficult questions

If you come across a difficult question, mark it with a paper clip (useful to have along) and come back to it when you have been through the booklet. One caution if you do this – be sure to skip a number on your answer sheet as well. Check often to be sure that you have not lost your place and that you are marking in the row numbered the same as the question you are answering.

6) Read the questions

Be sure you know what the question asks! Many capable people are unsuccessful because they failed to *read* the questions correctly.

7) Answer all questions

Unless you have been instructed that a penalty will be deducted for incorrect answers, it is better to guess than to omit a question.

8) Speed tests

It is often better NOT to guess on speed tests. It has been found that on timed tests people are tempted to spend the last few seconds before time is called in marking answers at random – without even reading them – in the hope of picking up a few extra points. To discourage this practice, the instructions may warn you that your score will be "corrected" for guessing. That is, a penalty will be applied. The incorrect answers will be deducted from the correct ones, or some other penalty formula will be used.

9) Review your answers

If you finish before time is called, go back to the questions you guessed or omitted to give them further thought. Review other answers if you have time.

10) Return your test materials

If you are ready to leave before others have finished or time is called, take ALL your materials to the monitor and leave quietly. Never take any test material with you. The monitor can discover whose papers are not complete, and taking a test booklet may be grounds for disqualification.

VIII. EXAMINATION TECHNIQUES

1) Read the general instructions carefully. These are usually printed on the first page of the exam booklet. As a rule, these instructions refer to the timing of the examination; the fact that you should not start work until the signal and must stop work at a signal, etc. If there are any *special* instructions, such as a choice of questions to be answered, make sure that you note this instruction carefully.

2) When you are ready to start work on the examination, that is as soon as the signal has been given, read the instructions to each question booklet, underline any key words or phrases, such as *least*, *best*, *outline*, *describe* and the like. In this way you will tend to answer as requested rather than discover on reviewing your paper that you *listed without describing*, that you selected the *worst* choice rather than the *best* choice, etc.

3) If the examination is of the objective or multiple-choice type – that is, each question will also give a series of possible answers: A, B, C or D, and you are called upon to select the best answer and write the letter next to that answer on your answer paper – it is advisable to start answering each question in turn. There may be anywhere from 50 to 100 such questions in the three or four hours allotted and you can see how much time would be taken if you read through all the questions before beginning to answer any. Furthermore, if you come across a question or group of questions which you know would be difficult to answer, it would undoubtedly affect your handling of all the other questions.

4) If the examination is of the essay type and contains but a few questions, it is a moot point as to whether you should read all the questions before starting to answer any one. Of course, if you are given a choice – say five out of seven and the like – then it is essential to read all the questions so you can eliminate the two that are most difficult. If, however, you are asked to answer all the questions, there may be danger in trying to answer the easiest one first because you may find that you will spend too much time on it. The best technique is to answer the first question, then proceed to the second, etc.

5) Time your answers. Before the exam begins, write down the time it started, then add the time allowed for the examination and write down the time it must be completed, then divide the time available somewhat as follows:
   - If 3-1/2 hours are allowed, that would be 210 minutes. If you have 80 objective-type questions, that would be an average of 2-1/2 minutes per question. Allow yourself no more than 2 minutes per question, or a total of 160 minutes, which will permit about 50 minutes to review.
   - If for the time allotment of 210 minutes there are 7 essay questions to answer, that would average about 30 minutes a question. Give yourself only 25 minutes per question so that you have about 35 minutes to review.

6) The most important instruction is to *read each question* and make sure you know what is wanted. The second most important instruction is to *time yourself properly* so that you answer every question. The third most important instruction is to *answer every question.* Guess if you have to but include something for each question. Remember that you will receive no credit for a blank and will probably receive some credit if you write something in answer to an essay question. If you guess a letter – say "B" for a multiple-choice question – you may have guessed right. If you leave a blank as an answer to a multiple-choice question, the examiners may respect your feelings but it will not add a point to your score. Some exams may penalize you for wrong answers, so in such cases *only,* you may not want to guess unless you have some basis for your answer.

7) Suggestions
   a. Objective-type questions
      1. Examine the question booklet for proper sequence of pages and questions
      2. Read all instructions carefully
      3. Skip any question which seems too difficult; return to it after all other questions have been answered
      4. Apportion your time properly; do not spend too much time on any single question or group of questions

5. Note and underline key words – *all, most, fewest, least, best, worst, same, opposite,* etc.
6. Pay particular attention to negatives
7. Note unusual option, e.g., unduly long, short, complex, different or similar in content to the body of the question
8. Observe the use of "hedging" words – *probably, may, most likely,* etc.
9. Make sure that your answer is put next to the same number as the question
10. Do not second-guess unless you have good reason to believe the second answer is definitely more correct
11. Cross out original answer if you decide another answer is more accurate; do not erase until you are ready to hand your paper in
12. Answer all questions; guess unless instructed otherwise
13. Leave time for review

b. Essay questions
   1. Read each question carefully
   2. Determine exactly what is wanted. Underline key words or phrases.
   3. Decide on outline or paragraph answer
   4. Include many different points and elements unless asked to develop any one or two points or elements
   5. Show impartiality by giving pros and cons unless directed to select one side only
   6. Make and write down any assumptions you find necessary to answer the questions
   7. Watch your English, grammar, punctuation and choice of words
   8. Time your answers; don't crowd material

8) Answering the essay question

Most essay questions can be answered by framing the specific response around several key words or ideas. Here are a few such key words or ideas:

M's: manpower, materials, methods, money, management
P's: purpose, program, policy, plan, procedure, practice, problems, pitfalls, personnel, public relations

a. Six basic steps in handling problems:
   1. Preliminary plan and background development
   2. Collect information, data and facts
   3. Analyze and interpret information, data and facts
   4. Analyze and develop solutions as well as make recommendations
   5. Prepare report and sell recommendations
   6. Install recommendations and follow up effectiveness

b. Pitfalls to avoid
   1. *Taking things for granted* – A statement of the situation does not necessarily imply that each of the elements is necessarily true; for example, a complaint may be invalid and biased so that all that can be taken for granted is that a complaint has been registered

2. *Considering only one side of a situation* – Wherever possible, indicate several alternatives and then point out the reasons you selected the best one
3. *Failing to indicate follow up* – Whenever your answer indicates action on your part, make certain that you will take proper follow-up action to see how successful your recommendations, procedures or actions turn out to be
4. *Taking too long in answering any single question* – Remember to time your answers properly

IX. AFTER THE TEST

Scoring procedures differ in detail among civil service jurisdictions although the general principles are the same. Whether the papers are hand-scored or graded by machine we have described, they are nearly always graded by number. That is, the person who marks the paper knows only the number – never the name – of the applicant. Not until all the papers have been graded will they be matched with names. If other tests, such as training and experience or oral interview ratings have been given, scores will be combined. Different parts of the examination usually have different weights. For example, the written test might count 60 percent of the final grade, and a rating of training and experience 40 percent. In many jurisdictions, veterans will have a certain number of points added to their grades.

After the final grade has been determined, the names are placed in grade order and an eligible list is established. There are various methods for resolving ties between those who get the same final grade – probably the most common is to place first the name of the person whose application was received first. Job offers are made from the eligible list in the order the names appear on it. You will be notified of your grade and your rank as soon as all these computations have been made. This will be done as rapidly as possible.

People who are found to meet the requirements in the announcement are called "eligibles." Their names are put on a list of eligible candidates. An eligible's chances of getting a job depend on how high he stands on this list and how fast agencies are filling jobs from the list.

When a job is to be filled from a list of eligibles, the agency asks for the names of people on the list of eligibles for that job. When the civil service commission receives this request, it sends to the agency the names of the three people highest on this list. Or, if the job to be filled has specialized requirements, the office sends the agency the names of the top three persons who meet these requirements from the general list.

The appointing officer makes a choice from among the three people whose names were sent to him. If the selected person accepts the appointment, the names of the others are put back on the list to be considered for future openings.

That is the rule in hiring from all kinds of eligible lists, whether they are for typist, carpenter, chemist, or something else. For every vacancy, the appointing officer has his choice of any one of the top three eligibles on the list. This explains why the person whose name is on top of the list sometimes does not get an appointment when some of the persons lower on the list do. If the appointing officer chooses the second or third eligible, the No. 1 eligible does not get a job at once, but stays on the list until he is appointed or the list is terminated.

X. HOW TO PASS THE INTERVIEW TEST

The examination for which you applied requires an oral interview test. You have already taken the written test and you are now being called for the interview test – the final part of the formal examination.

You may think that it is not possible to prepare for an interview test and that there are no procedures to follow during an interview. Our purpose is to point out some things you can do in advance that will help you and some good rules to follow and pitfalls to avoid while you are being interviewed.

What is an interview supposed to test?

The written examination is designed to test the technical knowledge and competence of the candidate; the oral is designed to evaluate intangible qualities, not readily measured otherwise, and to establish a list showing the relative fitness of each candidate – as measured against his competitors – for the position sought. Scoring is not on the basis of "right" and "wrong," but on a sliding scale of values ranging from "not passable" to "outstanding." As a matter of fact, it is possible to achieve a relatively low score without a single "incorrect" answer because of evident weakness in the qualities being measured.

Occasionally, an examination may consist entirely of an oral test – either an individual or a group oral. In such cases, information is sought concerning the technical knowledges and abilities of the candidate, since there has been no written examination for this purpose. More commonly, however, an oral test is used to supplement a written examination.

Who conducts interviews?

The composition of oral boards varies among different jurisdictions. In nearly all, a representative of the personnel department serves as chairman. One of the members of the board may be a representative of the department in which the candidate would work. In some cases, "outside experts" are used, and, frequently, a businessman or some other representative of the general public is asked to serve. Labor and management or other special groups may be represented. The aim is to secure the services of experts in the appropriate field.

However the board is composed, it is a good idea (and not at all improper or unethical) to ascertain in advance of the interview who the members are and what groups they represent. When you are introduced to them, you will have some idea of their backgrounds and interests, and at least you will not stutter and stammer over their names.

What should be done before the interview?

While knowledge about the board members is useful and takes some of the surprise element out of the interview, there is other preparation which is more substantive. It *is* possible to prepare for an oral interview – in several ways:

1) Keep a copy of your application and review it carefully before the interview

This may be the only document before the oral board, and the starting point of the interview. Know what education and experience you have listed there, and the sequence and dates of all of it. Sometimes the board will ask you to review the highlights of your experience for them; you should not have to hem and haw doing it.

2) Study the class specification and the examination announcement

Usually, the oral board has one or both of these to guide them. The qualities, characteristics or knowledges required by the position sought are stated in these documents. They offer valuable clues as to the nature of the oral interview. For example, if the job involves supervisory responsibilities, the announcement will usually indicate that knowledge of modern supervisory methods and the qualifications of the candidate as a supervisor will be tested. If so, you can expect such questions, frequently in the form of a hypothetical situation which you are expected to solve. NEVER go into an oral without knowledge of the duties and responsibilities of the job you seek.

3) Think through each qualification required

Try to visualize the kind of questions you would ask if you were a board member. How well could you answer them? Try especially to appraise your own knowledge and background in each area, *measured against the job sought*, and identify any areas in which you are weak. Be critical and realistic – do not flatter yourself.

4) Do some general reading in areas in which you feel you may be weak

For example, if the job involves supervision and your past experience has NOT, some general reading in supervisory methods and practices, particularly in the field of human relations, might be useful. Do NOT study agency procedures or detailed manuals. The oral board will be testing your understanding and capacity, not your memory.

5) Get a good night's sleep and watch your general health and mental attitude

You will want a clear head at the interview. Take care of a cold or any other minor ailment, and of course, no hangovers.

What should be done on the day of the interview?

Now comes the day of the interview itself. Give yourself plenty of time to get there. Plan to arrive somewhat ahead of the scheduled time, particularly if your appointment is in the fore part of the day. If a previous candidate fails to appear, the board might be ready for you a bit early. By early afternoon an oral board is almost invariably behind schedule if there are many candidates, and you may have to wait. Take along a book or magazine to read, or your application to review, but leave any extraneous material in the waiting room when you go in for your interview. In any event, relax and compose yourself.

The matter of dress is important. The board is forming impressions about you – from your experience, your manners, your attitude, and your appearance. Give your personal appearance careful attention. Dress your best, but not your flashiest. Choose conservative, appropriate clothing, and be sure it is immaculate. This is a business interview, and your appearance should indicate that you regard it as such. Besides, being well groomed and properly dressed will help boost your confidence.

Sooner or later, someone will call your name and escort you into the interview room. *This is it.* From here on you are on your own. It is too late for any more preparation. But remember, you asked for this opportunity to prove your fitness, and you are here because your request was granted.

What happens when you go in?

The usual sequence of events will be as follows: The clerk (who is often the board stenographer) will introduce you to the chairman of the oral board, who will introduce you to the other members of the board. Acknowledge the introductions before you sit down. Do not be surprised if you find a microphone facing you or a stenotypist sitting by. Oral interviews are usually recorded in the event of an appeal or other review.

Usually the chairman of the board will open the interview by reviewing the highlights of your education and work experience from your application – primarily for the benefit of the other members of the board, as well as to get the material into the record. Do not interrupt or comment unless there is an error or significant misinterpretation; if that is the case, do not hesitate. But do not quibble about insignificant matters. Also, he will usually ask you some question about your education, experience or your present job – partly to get you to start talking and to establish the interviewing "rapport." He may start the actual questioning, or turn it over to one of the other members. Frequently, each member undertakes the questioning on a particular area, one in which he is perhaps most competent, so you can expect each member to participate in the examination. Because time is limited, you may also expect some rather abrupt switches in the direction the questioning takes, so do not be upset by it. Normally, a board member will not pursue a single line of questioning unless he discovers a particular strength or weakness.

After each member has participated, the chairman will usually ask whether any member has any further questions, then will ask you if you have anything you wish to add. Unless you are expecting this question, it may floor you. Worse, it may start you off on an extended, extemporaneous speech. The board is not usually seeking more information. The question is principally to offer you a last opportunity to present further qualifications or to indicate that you have nothing to add. So, if you feel that a significant qualification or characteristic has been overlooked, it is proper to point it out in a sentence or so. Do not compliment the board on the thoroughness of their examination – they have been sketchy, and you know it. If you wish, merely say, "No thank you, I have nothing further to add." This is a point where you can "talk yourself out" of a good impression or fail to present an important bit of information. Remember, *you close the interview yourself.*

The chairman will then say, "That is all, Mr. ______, thank you." Do not be startled; the interview is over, and quicker than you think. Thank him, gather your belongings and take your leave. Save your sigh of relief for the other side of the door.

How to put your best foot forward

Throughout this entire process, you may feel that the board individually and collectively is trying to pierce your defenses, seek out your hidden weaknesses and embarrass and confuse you. Actually, this is not true. They are obliged to make an appraisal of your qualifications for the job you are seeking, and they want to see you in your best light. Remember, they must interview all candidates and a non-cooperative candidate may become a failure in spite of their best efforts to bring out his qualifications. Here are 15 suggestions that will help you:

1) Be natural – Keep your attitude confident, not cocky

If you are not confident that you can do the job, do not expect the board to be. Do not apologize for your weaknesses, try to bring out your strong points. The board is interested in a positive, not negative, presentation. Cockiness will antagonize any board member and make him wonder if you are covering up a weakness by a false show of strength.

2) Get comfortable, but don't lounge or sprawl

Sit erectly but not stiffly. A careless posture may lead the board to conclude that you are careless in other things, or at least that you are not impressed by the importance of the occasion. Either conclusion is natural, even if incorrect. Do not fuss with your clothing, a pencil or an ashtray. Your hands may occasionally be useful to emphasize a point; do not let them become a point of distraction.

3) Do not wisecrack or make small talk

This is a serious situation, and your attitude should show that you consider it as such. Further, the time of the board is limited – they do not want to waste it, and neither should you.

4) Do not exaggerate your experience or abilities

In the first place, from information in the application or other interviews and sources, the board may know more about you than you think. Secondly, you probably will not get away with it. An experienced board is rather adept at spotting such a situation, so do not take the chance.

5) If you know a board member, do not make a point of it, yet do not hide it

Certainly you are not fooling him, and probably not the other members of the board. Do not try to take advantage of your acquaintanceship – it will probably do you little good.

6) Do not dominate the interview

Let the board do that. They will give you the clues – do not assume that you have to do all the talking. Realize that the board has a number of questions to ask you, and do not try to take up all the interview time by showing off your extensive knowledge of the answer to the first one.

7) Be attentive

You only have 20 minutes or so, and you should keep your attention at its sharpest throughout. When a member is addressing a problem or question to you, give him your undivided attention. Address your reply principally to him, but do not exclude the other board members.

8) Do not interrupt

A board member may be stating a problem for you to analyze. He will ask you a question when the time comes. Let him state the problem, and wait for the question.

9) Make sure you understand the question

Do not try to answer until you are sure what the question is. If it is not clear, restate it in your own words or ask the board member to clarify it for you. However, do not haggle about minor elements.

10) Reply promptly but not hastily

A common entry on oral board rating sheets is "candidate responded readily," or "candidate hesitated in replies." Respond as promptly and quickly as you can, but do not jump to a hasty, ill-considered answer.

11) Do not be peremptory in your answers

A brief answer is proper – but do not fire your answer back. That is a losing game from your point of view. The board member can probably ask questions much faster than you can answer them.

12) Do not try to create the answer you think the board member wants

He is interested in what kind of mind you have and how it works – not in playing games. Furthermore, he can usually spot this practice and will actually grade you down on it.

13) Do not switch sides in your reply merely to agree with a board member

Frequently, a member will take a contrary position merely to draw you out and to see if you are willing and able to defend your point of view. Do not start a debate, yet do not surrender a good position. If a position is worth taking, it is worth defending.

14) Do not be afraid to admit an error in judgment if you are shown to be wrong

The board knows that you are forced to reply without any opportunity for careful consideration. Your answer may be demonstrably wrong. If so, admit it and get on with the interview.

15) Do not dwell at length on your present job

The opening question may relate to your present assignment. Answer the question but do not go into an extended discussion. You are being examined for a *new* job, not your present one. As a matter of fact, try to phrase ALL your answers in terms of the job for which you are being examined.

Basis of Rating

Probably you will forget most of these "do's" and "don'ts" when you walk into the oral interview room. Even remembering them all will not ensure you a passing grade. Perhaps you did not have the qualifications in the first place. But remembering them will help you to put your best foot forward, without treading on the toes of the board members.

Rumor and popular opinion to the contrary notwithstanding, an oral board wants you to make the best appearance possible. They know you are under pressure – but they also want to see how you respond to it as a guide to what your reaction would be under the pressures of the job you seek. They will be influenced by the degree of poise you display, the personal traits you show and the manner in which you respond.

ABOUT THIS BOOK

This book contains tests divided into Examination Sections. Go through each test, answering every question in the margin. We have also attached a sample answer sheet at the back of the book that can be removed and used. At the end of each test look at the answer key and check your answers. On the ones you got wrong, look at the right answer choice and learn. Do not fill in the answers first. Do not memorize the questions and answers, but understand the answer and principles involved. On your test, the questions will likely be different from the samples. Questions are changed and new ones added. If you understand these past questions you should have success with any changes that arise. Tests may consist of several types of questions. We have additional books on each subject should more study be advisable or necessary for you. Finally, the more you study, the better prepared you will be. This book is intended to be the last thing you study before you walk into the examination room. Prior study of relevant texts is also recommended. NLC publishes some of these in our Fundamental Series. Knowledge and good sense are important factors in passing your exam. Good luck also helps. So now study this Passbook, absorb the material contained within and take that knowledge into the examination. Then do your best to pass that exam.

EXAMINATION SECTION

EXAMINATION SECTION
TEST 1

DIRECTIONS: Each question or incomplete statement is followed by several suggested answers or completions. Select the one that BEST answers the question or completes the statement. *PRINT THE LETTER OF THE CORRECT ANSWER IN THE SPACE AT THE RIGHT.*

1. An employee under your supervision complains that he is assigned to work late more often than any of the other employees in the garage. You check the records and find that this isn't so. 1.____
You should

   A. advise this employee not to worry about what the other employees do but to see that he puts in a full day's work himself
   B. explain to this employee that you get the same complaint from all the other employees
   C. inform this employee that you have checked the records and the complaint is not justified
   D. not assign this employee to work late for a few days in order to keep him satisfied

2. A garage employee has reported late for work several times. 2.____
His supervisor should

   A. give this employee less desirable assignments
   B. overlook the lateness if the employee's work is otherwise exceptional
   C. recommend disciplinary action for habitual lateness
   D. talk the matter over with the employee before doing anything further

3. In choosing a man to be in charge in his absence, the supervisor should select first the employee who 3.____

   A. has ability to supervise others
   B. has been longest with the organization
   C. has the nicest appearance and manner
   D. is most skilled in his assigned duties

4. An employee under your supervision comes to you to complain about a decision you have made in assigning the men. He is excited and angry. You think what he is complaining about is not important, but it seems very important to him. 4.____
The BEST way for you to handle this is to

   A. let him talk until *he gets it off his chest* and then explain the reasons for your decision
   B. refuse to talk to him until he has cooled off
   C. show him at once how unimportant the matter is and how ridiculous his arguments are
   D. tell him to take it up with your superior if he disagrees with your decision

5. Suppose that a new employee has been appointed and assigned to your supervision. 5.____
When this man reports for work, it would be BEST for you to

A. ask him questions about different problems connected with a motor vehicle and see if he answers them correctly
B. check him carefully while he carries out some routine assignment that you give him
C. explain to him the general nature of the work he will be required to do
D. make a careful study of his previous work record before coming to the Department

6. The competent supervisor will be friendly with the employees under his supervision but will avoid close familiarity. 6.____
This statement is justified MAINLY because

A. a friendly attitude on the part of the supervisor toward the employee is likely to cause suspicion on the part of the employee
B. a supervisor can handle his employees better if he doesn't know their personal problems
C. close familiarity may interfere with the discipline needed for good supervisor-subordinate relationships
D. familiarity with the employees may be a sign of lack of ability on the part of the supervisor

7. An employee disagrees with the instructions that you, his supervisor, have given him for carrying out a certain assignment. 7.____
The BEST action for you to take is to tell this employee that

A. he can do what he wants but you will hold him responsible for failure
B. orders must be carried out or morale will fall apart
C. this job has been done in this way for many years with great success
D. you will be glad to listen to his objections and to his suggestions for improvement

8. As a supervisor, it is LEAST important for you to use a new employee's probationary period for the purpose of 8.____

A. carefully checking how he performs the work you assign him
B. determining whether he can perform the duties of his job efficiently
C. preparing him for promotion to a higher position
D. showing him how to carry out his assigned duties properly

9. Suppose you have just given an employee under your supervision instructions on how to carry out a certain assignment. 9.____
The BEST way to check that he has understood your instructions is to

A. ask him to repeat your instructions word for word
B. check the progress of his work the first chance you get
C. invite him to ask questions if he has any doubts
D. question him briefly about the main points of the assignment

10. Suppose you find it necessary to change a procedure that the men under your supervision have been following for a long time. 10.____
A good way to get their cooperation for this change would be to

A. bring them together to talk over the new procedure and explain the reasons for its adoption
B. explain to the men that if most of them still don't approve of the change after giving it a fair try, you will consider giving it up

C. give them a few weeks' notice of the proposed change in procedure
D. not enforce the new procedure strictly at the beginning

11. An order can be given by a supervisor in such a way as to make the employee want to obey it. 11.____
According to this statement, it is MOST reasonable to suppose that

A. a person will be glad to obey an order if he realizes that he must
B. if an order is given properly, it will be obeyed more willingly
C. it is easier to obey an order than to give one correctly
D. supervisors should inspire confidence by their actions as well as by their words

12. If one of the men you supervise disagrees with how you rate his work, the BEST way for you to handle this is to 12.____

A. advise him to appeal to your superior about it
B. decline to discuss the matter with him in order to keep discipline
C. explain why you rate him the way you do and talk it over with him
D. tell him that you are better qualified to rate his work than he is

13. A supervisor should be familiar with the experience and abilities of the employees under his supervision MAINLY because 13.____

A. each employee's work is highly important and requires a person of outstanding ability
B. it will help him to know which employees are best fitted for certain assignments
C. nearly all men have the same basic ability to do any job equally well
D. superior background shortly shows itself in superior work quality, regardless of assignment

14. The competent supervisor will try to develop respect rather than fear in his subordinates. 14.____
This statement is justified MAINLY because

A. fear is always present and, for best results, respect must be developed to offset it
B. it is generally easier to develop respect in the men than it is to develop fear
C. men who respect their supervisor are more likely to give more than the required minimum amount and quality of work
D. respect is based on the individual and fear is based on the organization as a whole

15. If one of the employees you supervise does outstanding work, you should 15.____

A. explain to him how his work can still be improved so that he will not become self-satisfied
B. mildly criticize the other men for not doing as good a job as this man
C. praise him for his work so that he will know it is appreciated
D. say nothing or he might become conceited

16. A supervisor can BEST help establish good morale among his employees if he 16.____

A. confides in them about his personal problems in order to encourage them to confide in him
B. encourages them to become friendly with him but discourages social engagements with them

C. points out to them the advantages of having a cooperative spirit in the department
D. sticks to the same rules that he expects them to follow

17. The one of the following situations which would seem to indicate poor scheduling of work by the supervisor in a garage is 17.____

A. everybody in the garage seeming to be very busy at the same time
B. re-assignment of a man to other work because of breakdown of a piece of equipment
C. two employees on vacation at the same time
D. two operators waiting to have their vehicles greased and the oil changed

Questions 18-20.

DIRECTIONS: Questions 18 through 20 are to be answered ONLY on the basis of the information given in the following paragraph.

The supervisor will gain the respect of the members of his staff and increase his influence over them by controlling his temper and avoiding criticizing anyone publicly. When a mistake is made, the good supervisor will talk it over with the employee quietly and privately. The supervisor will listen to the employee's story, suggest the better way of doing the job, and offer help so the mistake won't happen again. Before closing the discussion, the supervisor should try to find something good to say about other parts of the employee's work. Some praise and appreciation, along with instruction, is more likely to encourage an employee to improve in those areas where he is weakest.

18. A good title that would show the meaning of this entire paragraph would be 18.____

A. How to Correct Employee Errors
B. How to Praise Employees
C. Mistakes are Preventable
D. The Weak Employe

19. According to the above paragraph, the work of an employee who has made a mistake is more likely to improve if the supervisor 19.____

A. avoids criticizing him
B. gives him a chance to suggest a better way of doing the work
C. listens to the employee's excuses to see if he is right
D. praises good work at the same time he corrects the mistake

20. According to the above paragraph, when a supervisor needs to correct an employee's mistake, it is important that he 20.____

A. allow some time to go by after the mistake is made
B. do so when other employees are not present
C. show his influence with his tone of voice
D. tell other employees to avoid the same mistake

Questions 21-24.

DIRECTIONS: Questions 21 through 24 are to be answered ONLY on the basis of the information given in the following paragraph.

All automotive accidents, no matter how slight, are to be reported to the Safety Division by the employee involved on Accident Report Form S-23 in duplicate. When the accident is of such a nature that it requires the filling out of the State Motor Vehicle Report Form MV-104, this form is also prepared by the employee in duplicate and sent to the Safety Division for comparison with the Form S-23. The Safety Division forwards both copies of Form MV-104 to the Corporation Counsel, who sends one copy to the State Bureau of Motor Vehicles. When the information on the Form S-23 indicates that the employee may be at fault, an investigation is made by the Safety Division. If this investigation shows that the employee was at faulty the employee's dispatcher is asked to file a complaint on Form D-11. The foreman of mechanics prepares a damage report on Form D-8 and an estimate of the cost of repairs on Form D-9. The dispatcher's complaint, the damage report, the repair estimate, and the employee's previous accident record are sent to the Safety Division where they are studied together with the accident report. The Safety Division then recommends whether or not disciplinary action should be taken against the employee.

21. According to the above paragraph, the Safety Division should be notified whenever an automotive accident has occurred by means of 21.____

    A. Form S-23
    B. Forms S-23 and MV-104
    C. Forms S-23, MV-104, D-8, D-9, and D-11
    D. Forms S-23, MV-104, D-8, D-9, and D-11 and employee's accident report

22. According to the above paragraph, the forwarding of the Form MV-104 to the State Bureau of Motor Vehicles is done by the 22.____

    A. Corporation Counsel
    B. dispatcher
    C. employee involved in the accident
    D. Safety Division

23. According to the above paragraph, the Safety Division investigates an automotive accident if the 23.____

    A. accident is serious enough to be reported to the State Bureau of Motor Vehicles
    B. dispatcher files a complaint
    C. employee appears to have been at fault
    D. employee's previous accident report is poor

24. Of the forms mentioned in the above paragraph, the dispatcher is responsible for preparing the 24.____

    A. accident report form
    B. complaint form
    C. damage report
    D. estimate of cost of repairs

Questions 25-27.

DIRECTIONS: Questions 25 through 27 are to be answered ONLY on the basis of the information given in the following paragraph.

One of the major problems in the control of city motor equipment, and especially passenger equipment, is keeping the equipment working for the city and for the city alone for as many hours of the day as is practical. Even when most city employees try to get the most out of the cars, a poor system of control will result in wasted car hours. Some city employees have a legitimate use for a car all day long while others use a car only a small part of the day and then let it stand. As a rule, trucks are easier to control than passenger cars because they are usually assigned to a specific job where a foreman continually oversees them. Even though trucks are usually fully utilized, there are times when the normal work assignment cannot be carried out because of weather conditions or seasonal changes. At such times, a control system could plan to make the trucks available for other uses.

25. According to the above paragraph, a problem connected with controlling the use of city motor equipment is 25.____

    A. increasing the life span of the equipment
    B. keeping the equipment working all hours of the day
    C. preventing the over-use of the equipment to avoid breakdowns
    D. preventing the private use of the equipment

26. According to the above paragraph, a good control system for passenger equipment will MOST likely lead to 26.____

    A. better employees being assigned to operate the cars
    B. fewer city employees using city cars
    C. fewer wasted car hours for city cars
    D. insuring that city cars are used for legitimate purposes

27. According to the above paragraph, a control system for trucks is useful because 27.____

    A. a foreman usually supervises each job
    B. special conditions sometimes prevent the planned use of a truck
    C. trucks are easier to control than passenger cars
    D. trucks are usually assigned to specific jobs where they cannot be fully utilized

Questions 28-33.

DIRECTIONS: In the paragraph below, some of the underlined words have been purposely changed and spoil the meaning that the rest of the paragraph is meant to give. Read the paragraph carefully, then answer Questions 28 through 33.

The motor vehicle supervisor who is responsible for training drivers in the operation of special equipment cannot expect a man to carry out all of his duties poorly immediately after receiving instruction. The employee may be overwhelmed by all of the details he must master, happy because he is associated with new fellow workers, or fearful that he may not succeed on the job. It is the supervisor's job to make the operator feel at ease and discourage his self-confidence. The supervisor must also vary the speed of the driving according to the operator's capacity to absorb the instruction without undue pressure or confusion. All learners progress through several stages of development unless they become expert in their duties. As the operator's skills increase, he will require more instruction but the supervisor should be available to correct mistakes promptly to prevent wrong habits being formed.

28. Of the following words underlined in the above paragraph, the one that does NOT give the real meaning that the rest of the paragraph is meant to give is 28.____

A. responsible
B. special
C. happy
D. immediately

29. Of the following words underlined in the above paragraph, the one that does NOT give the real meaning that the rest of the paragraph is meant to give is 29.____

A. overwhelmed
B. happy
C. associated
D. succeed

30. Of the following words underlined in the above paragraph, the one that does NOT give the real meaning that the rest of the paragraph is meant to give is 30.____

A. job
B. operator
C. discourage
D. self-confidence

31. Of the following words underlined in the above paragraph, the one that does NOT give the real meaning that the rest of the paragraph is meant to give is 31.____

A. driving B. capacity C. absorb D. pressure

32. Of the following words underlined in the above paragraph, the one that does NOT give the real meaning that the rest of the paragraph is meant to give is 32.____

A. progress
B. several
C. development
D. unless

33. Of the following words underlined in the above paragraph, the one that does NOT give the real meaning that the rest of the paragraph is meant to give is 33.____

A. increase B. more C. mistakes D. habits

Questions 34-40.

DIRECTIONS: Each of Questions 34 through 40 consists of a word in capital letters followed by four suggested meanings of the word. Select the word or phrase which means MOST NEARLY the same as the word in capital letters.

34. ACCELERATE 34.____

A. adjust B. press C. quicken D. strip

35. ALIGN 35.____

A. bring into line
B. carry out
C. happen by chance
D. join together

36. CONTRACTION 36.____

A. agreement
B. denial
C. presentation
D. shrinkage

37. INTERVAL 37.____

A. ending
B. mixing together of
C. space of time
D. weaken

38. LUBRICATE 38.____

A. bend back
B. make slippery
C. rub out
D. soften

39. OBSOLETE 39.____

A. broken-down
B. hard to find
C. high-priced
D. out of date

40. RETARD 40.____

A. delay
B. flatten
C. rest
D. tally

KEY (CORRECT ANSWERS)

1. C	11. B	21. A	31. A
2. D	12. C	22. A	32. D
3. A	13. B	23. C	33. B
4. A	14. C	24. B	34. C
5. C	15. C	25. D	35. A
6. C	16. D	26. C	36. D
7. D	17. D	27. B	37. C
8. C	18. A	28. C	38. B
9. D	19. D	29. B	39. D
10. A	20. B	30. C	40. A

TEST 2

DIRECTIONS: Each question or incomplete statement is followed by several suggested answers or completions. Select the one that BEST answers the question or completes the statement. *PRINT THE LETTER OF THE CORRECT ANSWER IN THE SPACE AT THE RIGHT.*

Questions 1-3.

DIRECTIONS: Questions 1 through 3 consist of a word in capital letters followed by four suggested meanings of the word. Select the word or phrase which means MOST NEARLY the same as the word in capital letters.

1. SYNCHRONIZE 1.____

   A. draw out B. happen at the same time
   C. move at a steady rate D. turn smoothly

2. OSCILLATE 2.____

   A. attract B. echo C. roll D. swing

3. TERMINAL 3.____

   A. last B. moldy C. named D. spoken

4. In a certain garage, when the dispatcher issues gas and oil to a vehicle, he notes on his record the mileage reading of the vehicle. 4.____
   This is probably done MAINLY in order to

   A. check gas consumption against distance traveled
   B. compare age of vehicle with economy of operation
   C. decide when the vehicle should be scheduled for a grease job
   D. estimate future life expectancy of the vehicle

5. A supervisor of motor vehicle equipment was asked by the head of the bureau to investigate a certain procedure used in the garage and write a report with a recommendation whether the procedure should be changed. The supervisor, after he finished his investigation, made his report in which he said: *I recommend that you base your decision* to change the present procedure on whether or not the new procedure will improve operations. 5.____
   In this case, the supervisor carried out his assignment

   A. *poorly,* because he should have given his recommendation right at the beginning of the report
   B. *poorly,* because his investigation should have brought out whether the new procedure would improve operations
   C. *well,* because he left the final decision about changing the procedure up to the head of the bureau
   D. *well,* because he made an investigation and turned in a report as required

6. When a supervisor writes a report, it is LEAST important that 6.____

   A. all paragraphs in the report be of the same length
   B. a summary or list of the recommendations be given at the beginning of the report if the report is long
   C. independent ideas be taken up in separate paragraphs of the report
   D. the report give all the evidence on which the conclusions are based

7. The supervisor who makes a special point of using long words in preparing written reports is, in general, PROBABLY being 7.____

   A. *unwise,* because a written report should be factual and accurate
   B. *unwise,* because simplicity in a report is usually desirable
   C. *wise,* because the written report will become a permanent record
   D. *wise,* because with long words he can use the right emphasis in his report

8. The most thorough investigation is of no value if the report written by the person who made the investigation does not help his superior to decide what action to take. According to this statement, it is LEAST correct to suppose that 8.____

   A. an investigation is of no value unless it is thorough
   B. a purpose of the report turned in after an investigation is to help supervisors decide what action to take
   C. the report on an investigation is usually written by the person who made the investigation
   D. the value of an investigation depends in part on the report turned in

9. Before you turn in a report you have written of an investigation that you made, you discover some additional information that you didn't know about before. Whether or not you rewrite your report to include this additional information should depend MAINLY on the 9.____

   A. amount of time left in which to submit the report
   B. effect this information will have on the conclusions of the report
   C. number of changes that you will have to make in your original report
   D. possibility of turning in a supplementary report later

10. The advantage of using an *inspection check sheet* when making inspections of premises or equipment is that 10.____

   A. fewer inspections are required
   B. the inspection becomes easy and can be done by a subordinate
   C. there is less chance of forgetting some important point of the inspection
   D. there is less paper work

11. Of the following methods for keeping supplies and records of supplies, the one that will MOST quickly tell you at any time how many pieces of any item are on hand in the supply room is 11.____

   A. keeping a minimum number of each item on hand
   B. recording each item when it is added to or removed from stock
   C. stocking the same number of pieces of each item and reordering weekly to keep the count even
   D. taking a daily count

12. When a supervisor submits a report on a motor vehicle accident, it is LEAST important for him to include in his report the 12.____

A. addresses of the witnesses to the accident
B. number of the police precinct where the accident happened
C. probable cause of the accident
D. time of the accident

13. The MAIN reason a supervisor in charge of motor vehicle equipment or personnel should make sure that his men obey the safety rules is that 13.____

A. accident prevention is a new program and should be tried out
B. every accident can be prevented
C. other safety measures are not needed where safety rules are obeyed
D. safety rules are based on proven methods of accident prevention

14. When he investigates an accident in which a city vehicle was involved, the MAIN object of the supervisor should be to 14.____

A. complete the investigation as fast as possible
B. determine if the city operator's record is so bad that he should be fired
C. get all the facts to establish the cause of the accident
D. try to establish that the other driver was at least equally to blame

15. If witnesses to an automobile accident are interviewed separately, they are more likely to give different versions of the circumstances of the accident than if they are interviewed together. 15.____
According to this statement, it is MOST probable that

A. a truer picture of the circumstances of an accident can be gotten by interviewing the witnesses together rather than separately
B. a witness's impression of what he saw is influenced by the statement of the other witnesses as to what they saw
C. people who see an accident as a group will agree about the details of the accident more than people who are not together when they see the accident
D. witnesses are less likely to tell the truth when interviewed privately than when interviewed as a group

16. A thorough investigation should always be made of an accident in which a city vehicle is involved. 16.____
The MAIN value of such an investigation is to

A. discover any factors that contributed to the accident which may be corrected
B. keep compensation claims down
C. provide good records from which statistics can be developed
D. show the operators that accidents are taken seriously, no matter how small

17. An accident has been described as *an unplanned event caused by an unsafe act or condition.* 17.____
An example of an unsafe act, rather than of an unsafe condition, in a garage is

A. blocked fire exits
B. defective tools or equipment
C. horseplay or teasing
D. oil and grease on floors

18. Of the following rules, the one that is LEAST directly concerned with the prevention of accidents is: 18.____

A. Check brake fluid before leaving garage
B. Do not use garage equipment if safety devices do not work
C. No smoking in garage
D. Reports of time lost due to accident must be submitted in 5 days

19. Which of the following entries on a Department Accident Report Form is MAINLY for the purpose of showing what is being done so that this type of accident will not happen again? 19.____

A. Describe accident, including vehicle or vehicles involved
B. What are you doing to prevent similar accidents?
C. Why did the unsafe condition exist?
D. Why was the unsafe act committed?

20. With respect to motor vehicle accidents, it is necessary to report in duplicate to the Bureau of Motor Vehicles on its printed forms 20.____

A. all accidents
B. only those accidents in which someone is killed or injured
C. only those accidents in which someone is killed or injured or there is property damage of more than $50
D. only those accidents in which someone is killed or injured or there is property damage of more than $100

21. A section of a garage used for parking vehicle measures 162 1/2' x 25 3/4'. 21.____
If each vehicle to be parked in this section requires, on the average, 84 sq.ft. of parking space, the MAXIMUM number of vehicles that can be parked in this section is CLOSEST to

A. 50 B. 45 C. 40 D. 35

22. Each of the 23 vehicles in a garage uses an average of 114 gallons of gas every 4 weeks. 22.____
If the motor vehicle dispatcher is required to re-order gas when the gas tank in the garage shows no more than a one week supply, he MUST re-order when the gas tank shows ______ gallons.

A. 655 B. 705 C. 830 D. 960

23. An employee's annual salary is $45,800. His total and annual deductions are 22% for withholding tax, 8 1/2% for pension and social security, and $1,820 for health insurance. 23.____
The take-home pay that this employee would get on the check he receives every other week is MOST NEARLY

A. $577.10 B. $845.00 C. $1,154.20 D. $1,220.40

24. A vehicle which averages 14 1/2 miles to a gallon of gas uses a quart of oil for every 21 1/2 gallons of gas. 24.____
If the vehicle traveled 19,952 miles in a year, its oil consumption for the year would be ______ quarts.

A. 52 B. 56 C. 60 D. 64

25. Thirteen percent of all the vehicles in a certain garage are trucks. If there are 26 trucks, then the number of vehicles of other types in this garage is 25.____

A. 174 B. 200 C. 260 D. 338

26. Of 12 employees in a garage, four earn $3,500 a year, two earn $3,150 a year, one earns $4,550 a year, and the rest each earn $3,800 a year. 26.____
The average yearly salary of these employees is CLOSEST to

A. $3,550 B. $3,650 C. $3,750 D. $3,850

27. A garage bin used for storing supplies and parts measures 1 yard x 2 yards x 7 feet. 27.____
The cubic volume of this bin is

A. 5 1/3 cubic yards
B. 16 cubic feet
C. 63 cubic feet
D. 126 cubic feet

28. A garage has a gas tank with a capacity of 1,300 gallons. If there are only 520 gallons of gas in the tank, then the tank is _______ full. 28.____

A. 40% B. 33 1/3% C. 25% D. 16 3/4%

29. Of a specially selected group of vehicles, 1/5 are 6 months old, 2/5 are 12 months old, and 2/5 are 15 months old. 29.____
The average age of this group of vehicles is _______ months.

A. 9 B. 10 C. 11 D. 12

30. A suggestion has been made that every vehicle have its gas tank filled and oil and water checked when it returns to the garage at the end of the day. 30.____
This suggestion is

A. *good,* mainly because the gas pump can be kept locked the rest of the day
B. *good,* mainly because vehicles will be ready to go out promptly the next day
C. *poor,* mainly because it would take too long to fill each vehicle
D. *poor,* mainly because not every vehicle will need gas, oil, and water

31. Brakes do not generally have to be adjusted until the clearance between the bottom of the brake pedal and the floorboard goes below _______ inch(es). 31.____

A. 2-2 1/2 B. 1 1/2-2 C. 1-1 1/2 D. 1/2-1

32. *Play* in the steering wheel is generally NOT considered to be excessive until it reaches about _______ inch(es). 32.____

A. 1/2 B. 1 C. 1 1/2 D. 2

33. If the oil pressure gauge in a sedan reads unduly high even after the engine is warmed up, the MOST probable reason is 33.____

A. a low oil level in the crankcase
B. an internal leak in the oil system
C. an obstruction in the oil line
D. too light an oil being used

34. In order to keep tire pressure at the level recommended by the manufacturer, the air pressure in the tires should be 34.___

A. checked at the end of the day's driving
B. checked in the morning, before the vehicle is driven
C. lower in summer than in winter
D. reduced before a long trip to leave room for expansion

35. When inspecting one of your vehicles, you notice excessive wear on the center of the tread of both front tires. 35.___
This unusual wear is MOST likely caused by

A. excessive toe-in of the front wheels
B. over-inflation of the front tires
C. too much camber of the front wheels
D. under-inflation of the front tires

36. The level of the fluid in the battery should be ______ the top of the plates. 36.___

A. barely covering
B. exactly even with
C. well below
D. well over

37. A heavy layer of oil on the water in the radiator would MOST probably indicate a 37.___

A. cracked block
B. dirty air cleaner
C. loose hose connection
D. water pump leak

38. If a five gallon can of gasoline is spilled on the garage floor, the BEST action to take is to 38.___

A. let the gasoline evaporate
B. pour sand over the puddle of gasoline
C. squirt a foam-producing fire extinguisher on the puddle
D. use a hose to flush the gasoline away

39. Greasy rags and waste in a garage should be 39.___

A. hung up on a line to air out
B. put in boxes that will be emptied daily
C. put in covered metal cans or barrels
D. put in wire baskets outside the garage

40. Adjusting the carburetor to give a mixture that is richer in fuel is 40.___

A. *good* practice in cold weather as it improves engine operation
B. *good* practice in very hot weather as it prevents stalling
C. *poor* practice as it increases the chance of vapor lock
D. *poor* practice in stop-and-go city driving as it greatly increases gas consumption

KEY (CORRECT ANSWERS)

1.	B	11.	B	21.	A	31.	C
2.	D	12.	B	22.	A	32.	D
3.	A	13.	D	23.	C	33.	C
4.	A	14.	C	24.	D	34.	B
5.	B	15.	B	25.	A	35.	B
6.	A	16.	A	26.	B	36.	D
7.	B	17.	C	27.	D	37.	A
8.	A	18.	D	28.	A	38.	D
9.	B	19.	B	29.	D	39.	C
10.	C	20.	D	30.	B	40.	A

TEST 3

DIRECTIONS: Each question or incomplete statement is followed by several suggested answers or completions. Select the one that BEST answers the question or completes the statement. *PRINT THE LETTER OF THE CORRECT ANSWER IN THE SPACE AT THE RIGHT.*

Questions 1-10.

DIRECTIONS: Questions 1 through 10 are based on the information given in the map on page 2.

1. On pay day, you assign an operator to deliver paychecks by car to the four work crews assigned to street jobs in the area. He starts from the garage and is to return there when finished. 1.____
The order of delivery that would take the operator over the shortest allowable route would be crew

A. 1, 2, 3, 4
B. 2, 1, 4, 3
C. 3, 2, 1, 4
D. 4, 3, 2, 1

2. Work crew 4 will be finished with its job at 1 P.M. and has to be moved to a new work location at Fir Ave. and 5th St. Work crew 3 will be finished with its job at the same time and has to be moved to begin work on a new job at 6th St. and Elm Ave. The operator assigned to the truck is to start from and return to the garage. 2.____
In order to get each of these crews to their new locations as soon as possible, the dispatcher should instruct the operator assigned to pick up crew

A. 3 and drop them at their new location; then pick up crew 4 and drop them at their new location
B. 4 and drop them at their new location; pick up crew 3 and drop them at their new location
C. 3; pick up crew 4; drop off crew 3; drop off crew 4
D. 4; pick up crew 3; drop off crew 3; drop off crew 4

3. The shortest allowable route for driving from the repair shop to the garage is 2nd Street and 3.____

A. Fir Ave.
B. Gladiola Ave.
C. Gladiola Ave., 3rd St., Fir Ave.
D. Holly Ave., 1st St., Gladiola Ave.

4. You have requests for the following pick-ups and deliveries: a record player and loudspeaker to be moved from the playground to the skating rink, a case of pictures to be taken from the museum to the high school, and a ticket box to be moved from the stadium to the skating rink. 4.____
Using the shortest allowable route from the garage and back, the order in which these pick-ups and deliveries should be made with the LEAST number of stops is

A. museum, high school, playground, skating rink, stadium
B. museum, playground, high school, stadium, skating rink
C. playground, skating rink, museum, high school, stadium
D. stadium, skating rink, museum, high school, playground

A ◯ indicates a street work crew.

A ✕ indicates a an entrance.

Arrows on streets indicate one-way and two-way streets.
No U turns are permitted.

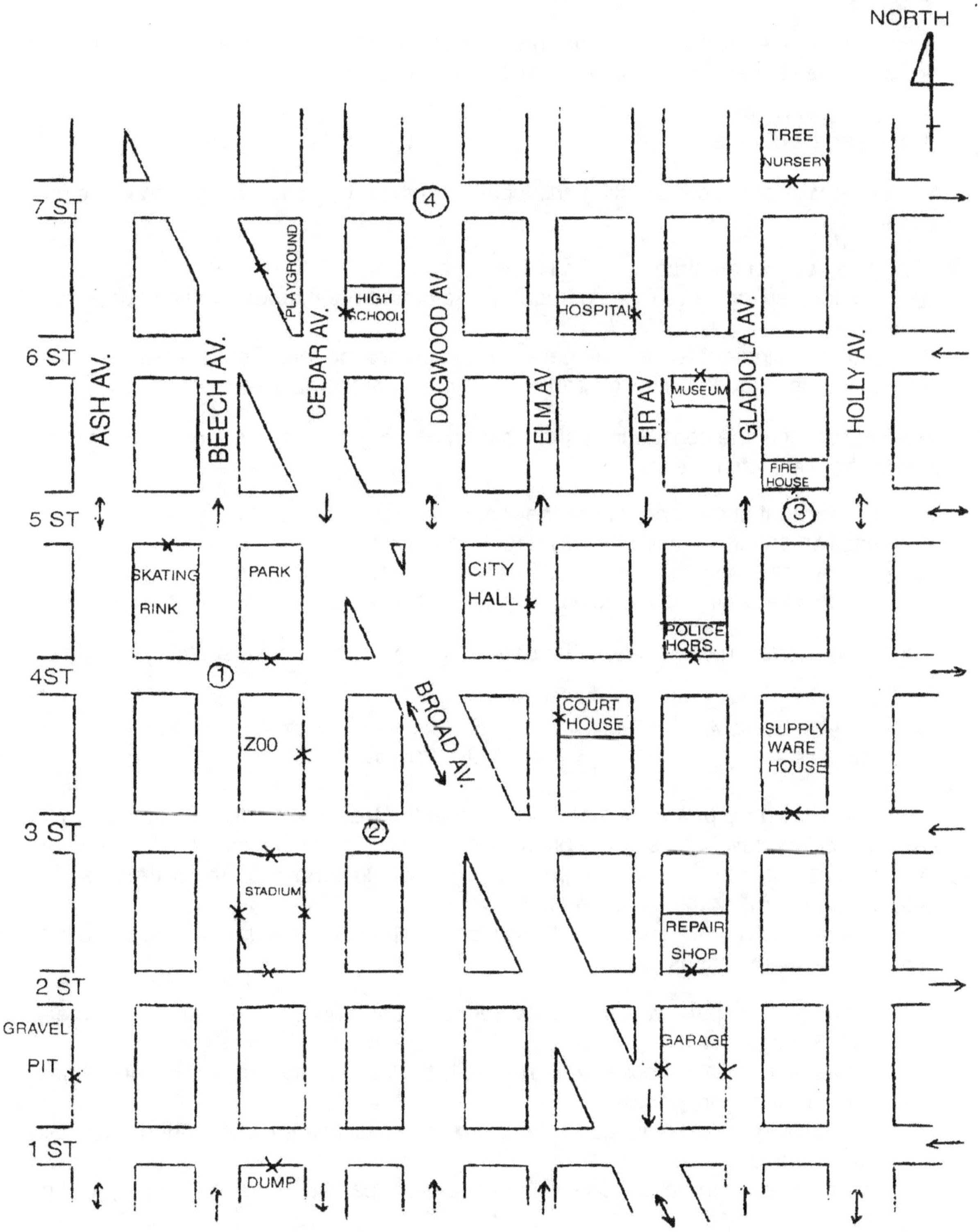

5. To help a newly assigned motor vehicle operator learn this area, you might ask him to study the direction of traffic patterns on the map. 5.___
It would be MOST helpful if you pointed out to him that two-way traffic is permitted on

A. all but one of the numbered streets
B. all but three of the named avenues
C. only one of the numbered streets
D. only three of the named avenues

6. In routing motor equipment to the northwestern part of the mapped area, the dispatcher would be wise to use Broad Avenue MAINLY because it is 6.___

A. a two-way street
B. a wide street
C. near the garage
D. the most direct route

7. A disadvantage of the construction and location of the repair shop, according to the map, is that 7.___

A. it has only one entrance on 2nd St.
B. it is located too close to the garage as equipment breakdowns would happen in the field
C. motor equipment leaving the garage must go around the block to enter the shop
D. the shop is too small in comparison to the size of the garage

8. Two factors about the construction and location of the garage that are of special advantage to the dispatcher are that it 8.___

A. has two entrances and is near the repair shop
B. has two entrances and one-way streets on all sides
C. is near the repair shop and occupies a whole block
D. occupies a whole block and has one-way streets on all sides

9. When dispatching equipment from the garage to the hospital, the dispatcher should use the entrance on 9.___

A. either Gladiola Ave. or Fir Ave.
B. Fir Ave.
C. Gladiola Ave.
D. 2nd St.

10. You have requests to pick up some small trees at the tree nursery to be delivered to the park, to pick up gravel at the gravel pit and deliver the load to the zoo, to take some broken benches from the park to the repair shop, to pick up supplies at the warehouse for delivery to City Hall and the court house. 10.___
The order in which a truck should do these jobs, starting from the garage and using the shortest allowable route is

A. gravel pit, zoo; park, repair shop; warehouse, court house, City Hall; tree nursery, park, garage
B. gravel pit, zoo; warehouse, court house, City Hall; tree nursery, park; park, repair shop; repair shop, garage
C. tree nursery, park; park, repair shop; zoo, gravel pit; warehouse, court house, City Hall, garage
D. warehouse, court house, City Hall; tree nursery, park; park, repair shop; gravel pit, zoo; zoo, garage

Questions 11-20.

DIRECTIONS: Answer Questions 11 through 20 ONLY on the basis of the information given below in the two charts and the Rules of the Department. You are to assume that you are the dispatcher in the garage where these charts are kept and where they are used in making daily assignments of operators and vehicles.

SECOND AVE. GARAGE MOTOR VEHICLE OPERATOR CONTROL SHEET Date: May 25, 19 __				SECOND AVE. GARAGE MOTOR VEHICLE OPERATOR CONTROL SHEET Date: May 25, 19 __			
Name of Operator	Cleared on	Hours of Overtime Credit as of May 25	On Vaca-tion	Vehicle Number and Type	In Re-pair Shop as of May 25	Date Due in Shop for Pre-ventive Mainten-ance In-spection	Date Last In Repair
Allen	P T	74		20-P		7/13	3/2
Boyd	P W	31	5/18-30	21-P		6/15	2/16
Cohen	P T	129		22-T		5/26	1/19
Diggs	P	15		23-P		6/1	5/8
Egan	P T	92	6/1-13	24-P		6/8	2/2
First	P T W	49		25-P		7/6	2/24
Gordon	P	57		26-W		6/1	1/21
Hanson	P T	143	6/15-27	27-T		7/20	4/6
				28-T	X	7/27	3/16
				29-P	X	5/18	1/12

Symbols: P - Passenger Car
T - Truck
W - Wrecker

Symbols: P - Passenger Car
T - Truck
W - Wrecker

RULES OF THE DEPARTMENT

1. A motor vehicle operator may be assigned to drive only those types of vehicles on which he has been cleared. No one but a motor vehicle operator may be assigned to drive a Department vehicle.

2. Private cars may not be used for Department business.

3. The motor vehicle dispatcher shall keep a daily record of overtime credits of all operators under his supervision to be sure that no operator acquires more than 150 hours of overtime credit. An assignment which involves overtime should be given, wherever possible, to the operator with the least overtime credit.

4. A vehicle due for preventive maintenance must be sent to the repair shop on the date it is due for preventive maintenance, except when a vehicle has been in the repair shop during the previous month.

5. All available vehicles are to be assigned to jobs as requested, with none held in reserve.

11. An official who is requesting a truck and operator for the three days beginning May 26th indicates to you that some overtime may be necessary for the operator, but he cannot predict how many hours of overtime will be needed. Under these circumstances, the MOST logical man for you to choose for this assignment would be operator 11.___

A. Allen B. Boyd C. Diggs D. First

12. The vehicle which does NOT have to be sent to the shop for preventive maintenance on the date it is due is vehicle number 12.___

A. 23 B. 25 C. 27 D. 29

13. As dispatcher, you receive a request on May 25th for a truck and motor vehicle operator for a job that will take three days, from May 26th through May 28th.
The vehicle that it would be BEST for you to choose on May 25th for this assignment is vehicle number 13.___

A. 28 B. 27 C. 22 D. 20

14. On May 25th, right after all the vehicles have left the garage on daily assignment, you receive a call from your Commissioner's secretary. She tells you that an emergency has come up and asks you for a car to be ready in fifteen minutes to take a messenger with important papers to be delivered to the Commissioner who is waiting for the papers at a court in another borough.
Of the following, the BEST thing for you to do, after explaining to the secretary that you have no cars available, is to 14.___

A. advise her she should give you advance notice the next time so that you can reserve a car for the messenger
B. offer to drive the messenger yourself in your private car
C. promise to get a car from another department
D. suggest that the messenger use public transportation

15. To give you more leeway in assigning your operators to the available equipment, it would be MOST practical for you to 15.___

A. ask your supervisor to assign two additional motor vehicle operators to the garage
B. have additional operators cleared on the wrecker
C. suggest to your supervisor that rule 3 be abolished
D. suggest to your supervisor that rule 1 be abolished

16. Other things being equal, the operator who should probably be of MOST value to you, as the dispatcher, is 16.___

A. Cohen B. Diggs C. First D. Hanson

17. The factor which indicates MOST strongly that there may not be enough operators assigned to this garage is the 17.___

A. amount of overtime accumulated
B. excess of number of vehicles over number of operators
C. incomplete vacation schedule
D. number of operators cleared on trucks

18. When dispatching men and equipment in the morning, it would be BEST for you to first dispatch men who 18.____

    A. are cleared on 1 vehicle
    B. are cleared on 2 vehicles
    C. are cleared on 3 vehicles
    D. have already had their vacations

19. The second week in June, you receive a call for an operator and wrecker. It is better to dispatch Boyd rather than First because 19.____

    A. he has already had his vacation
    B. he has less overtime
    C. he is not cleared on trucks
    D. unless there are special reasons, you might as well assign the men in alphabetical order for easier record keeping

20. You have requests for 6 passenger cars and 2 trucks for jobs on May 25th. All of these jobs will probably take the full day but none will require any overtime. How many of these requests for May 25th would you have to refuse? 20.____

    A. None
    B. One
    C. Two
    D. More than two

KEY (CORRECT ANSWERS)

1. B	11. D
2. A	12. A
3. D	13. B
4. B	14. D
5. C	15. B
6. D	16. C
7. C	17. A
8. A	18. A
9. C	19. C
10. B	20. B

TEST 4

DIRECTIONS: Each question or incomplete statement is followed by several suggested answers or completions. Select the one that BEST answers the question or completes the statement. *PRINT THE LETTER OF THE CORRECT ANSWER IN THE SPACE AT THE RIGHT.*

1. In a program of switching tires on a vehicle at regular intervals to give longer tire life, the BEST system to follow is 1.____

A. 
B. 
C. 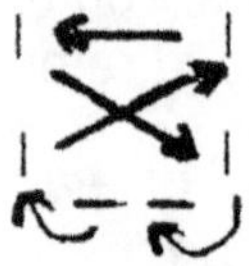
D. 

2. If an engine misfires when it is operated at low speed, the order in which the items below should be inspected, tested, and adjusted is 2.____

   A. breaker contact points, distributor cap and rotor, high voltage wires, spark plugs
   B. distributor cap and rotor, breaker contact points, spark plugs, high voltage wires
   C. high voltage wires, spark plugs, breaker contact points, distributor can and rotor
   D. spark plugs, high voltage wires, distributor cap and rotor, breaker contact points

3. An operator complains that the headlights on his vehicle flare up and then dim as the speed of the vehicle changes. 3.____
The MOST probable cause is

   A. a burned out fuse or defective circuit breaker
   B. a defective dimmer switch
   C. a loose connection in the headlight wiring
   D. weak bulbs

4. A can of motor oil is marked *S.A.E. 20-20W* 4.____
This indicates that

   A. a mistake was made, and the oil should not be used
   B. chemicals have been added to winterize the oil
   C. the oil may be used both in medium temperatures and in winter weather
   D. the oil should be used when the temperature is between 20 degrees below and 20 degrees above zero

5. A specific gravity reading of 1280 at 80° F means that a battery is 5.____

   A. fully discharged
   B. nearing a discharged condition
   C. about half charged
   D. fully charged

6. If a generator constantly charges at a high rate, it is MOST probably due to a(n) 6.____

   A. defective regulator
   B. dirty commutator
   C. too tight fan belt adjustment
   D. overcharged battery

7. In the servicing of spark plugs, it is IMPORTANT to 7.____

A. bend the center electrode rather than the side electrode when adjusting the spark plug gap
B. clean the spark plug recess in the cylinder head with a brush or compressed air after a spark plug has been removed
C. make sure that each spark plug has only one gasket
D. use an adjustable wrench to tighten a spark plug in its hole

8. If air gets into the lines of a hydraulic brake system, the MOST likely result will be 8.____

A. a spongy pedal
B. grabbing brakes
C. locked brakes
D. a hard pedal

9. In hooking test ammeters and voltmeters into a circuit, the ammeter 9.____

A. should be connected in parallel and the voltmeter in series
B. should be connected in series and the voltmeter in parallel
C. and voltmeter should be connected in parallel
D. and voltmeter should be connected in series

10. When brakes are correctly adjusted but one wheel takes hold before the others, it is MOST likely that the 10.____

A. cup on the wheel cylinder has swelled
B. relief port on the master cylinder isn't working
C. push rod adjustment is faulty
D. brake fluid has leaked into the lining

11. Racing an automobile engine on cold mornings to warm it up is 11.____

A. *bad* practice, because there is poor lubrication of moving parts
B. *good* practice, because the oil will reach moving parts faster
C. *bad* practice, because it will form sludge in the engine
D. *good* practice, because it will allow liquid gasoline to reach the crankcase

12. Using anti-freeze solution for more than a single season is 12.____

A. *bad* practice, because it will cause excessive rust
B. *good* practice, because it will be economical
C. *bad* practice, because it will raise the boiling point
D. *good* practice, because it will not clog the cooling system

13. The one of the following which is NOT usually a purpose of a preventive maintenance program for a fleet of automotive vehicles is 13.____

A. a greater margin of safety in the operation of the vehicles
B. easier and more comfortable driving
C. improved mechanical ability of vehicle operators
D. increased economy in vehicle operations

14. The one of the following which will NOT help improve gasoline mileage is 14.____

A. driving at high speeds
B. even acceleration
C. keeping tires at recommended pressure
D. using light oil in winter

15. An abnormally cool brake drum on one wheel after the vehicle has been in operation would MOST probably indicate a(n) 15.____

A. dragging shoe
B. improperly adjusted brake drum
C. non-functioning brake
D. underlubricated bearing

16. The pitman arm is part of the 16.____

A. brake shoe assembly
B. driving axle
C. fan belt assembly
D. steering mechanism

17. When he returns to the garage at the end of his shift, a motor vehicle operator complains to you that the engine *skips* on the car he is driving. 17.____
When you prepare your requisition for a check-up of this vehicle, it is LEAST important for you to ask for a check of the

A. battery
B. carburetor
C. condenser
D. fuel line

18. In a garage where a vehicle preventive maintenance program is in operation, the one of the following which it is MOST important to do right away without waiting for next checkup is 18.____

A. adjusting brakes that pull unevenly
B. changing oil and lubrication to summer or winter grades
C. checking spark plugs
D. replacing an oil-soaked water hose

19. To test whether every cylinder has good compression, the instrument that should be used is a 19.____

A. vacuum gauge
B. gas analyzer
C. creeper
D. vent ball

20. It is generally recommended that the radiator of a passenger vehicle be flushed out 20.____

A. every 1,000 miles
B. every fall and spring
C. every 2,000 miles
D. once a year

KEY (CORRECT ANSWERS)

1.	A	11.	A
2.	D	12.	A
3.	C	13.	C
4.	C	14.	A
5.	D	15.	C
6.	A	16.	D
7.	C	17.	A
8.	A	18.	A
9.	B	19.	A
10.	D	20.	B

EXAMINATION SECTION
TEST 1

DIRECTIONS: Each question or incomplete statement is followed by several suggested answers or completions. Select the one that BEST answers the question or completes the statement. *PRINT THE LETTER OF THE CORRECT ANSWER IN THE SPACE AT THE RIGHT.*

1. Suppose that a new motor vehicle operator has been assigned to you, the dispatcher. It is your responsibility to see that he understands how to fill out the forms he is required to use. 1.____
Of the following, the BEST way to do this would be to

   A. ask an experienced driver to tell him about the forms
   B. explain the purpose of each form to the new operator, and show him how to fill them out
   C. give the new man a copy of each form, so that he can study them
   D. tell the new man that filling out forms is simple, and that he should just follow the instructions on each form

2. As a dispatcher, you may from time to time be faced with an important job problem. 2.____
The usual way of solving a job problem includes the following four steps:
   I. Seeing what the facts mean in relation to the problem
   II. Choosing the best solution
   III. Getting all the important facts relating to the problem
   IV. Finding possible solutions

   If the above four numbered steps were arranged in the order in which they should be taken, the CORRECT order would be

   A. IV, III, I, II
   B. IV, I, III, II
   C. III, I, IV, II
   D. I, IV, III, II

3. Of the following, it is LEAST desirable that a dispatcher 3.____

   A. correct a driver for a minor rule violation, even if it is the first time that the driver broke the rule and no harm was done
   B. discuss with any new drivers he supervises some situations that may come up in their work and how to handle them
   C. encourage the drivers he supervises to ask him questions about any of his instructions that they do not understand
   D. observe for a few days the mistakes one of his drivers makes and then discuss these mistakes with him

4. Suppose you receive a telephone call from an employee who complains that, while being driven on official business, he was treated rudely by the driver. 4.____
As the dispatcher who supervises this driver, which of the following actions should you take FIRST?

   A. Tell the caller that you will have the driver write him a letter of apology
   B. Tell the caller that you will have the driver telephone him to apologize
   C. Ask the other drivers you supervise if this driver is generally discourteous
   D. Try to get the details of the incident from the caller and from the driver

5. When a certain dispatcher has to criticize one of his drivers, he makes a practice of doing it in private. 5.____
This practice is GENERALLY

A. *good;* private criticism can help save the driver unnecessary embarrassment
B. *bad;* open criticism helps develop among the drivers a feeling of being treated fairly
C. *good;* private criticism leaves no hard feelings between the driver and the dispatcher
D. *bad;* open criticism keeps the drivers on their toes

6. A certain dispatcher often issues orders in the form of a request rather than in the form of a command. 6.____
This is

A. *good;* it lets the driver decide the best way to carry out such an order
B. *poor;* it shows that the dispatcher lacks sufficient self-confidence
C. *good;* it helps to create good will with the drivers
D. *poor;* it puts the responsibility on the drivers to decide which job to do first

7. For a dispatcher to judge the performance of a driver exclusively on how well he drives, his safety record, and his neatness of appearance would be 7.____

A. *undesirable;* there are other important factors to consider also
B. *desirable;* these factors are objective and eliminate personal bias
C. *undesirable;* these factors should have been judged before the driver was appointed
D. *desirable;* this method stresses on-the-job performance

8. Suppose you discover that you have unfairly criticized one of the drivers you supervise. 8.____
Of the following, the BEST thing for you to do would be to

A. think of some indirect way to let the driver know you realize that he was not at fault
B. admit your mistake to the driver, and apologize
C. overlook some offense that the driver commits in the future
D. make up for it by giving this driver better assignments for a short time

9. A driver, who otherwise does a rather good job, is starting to arrive late for work too often. You, as the dispatcher, have called him in to talk to him about it. 9.____
Which of the following would be BEST for you to do?

A. Let him know right away that there are no excuses for being late this much
B. Discuss these latenesses with him but also mention good points in his work
C. Give him a strong warning of punishment in order to stop the habit right away
D. Tell him that he ought to improve to keep the other drivers from complaining

10. A year ago you corrected one of the men you supervise for driving carelessly while in the garage. Since then he has been careful not to repeat such actions. 10.____
To remind this driver once in a while about that careless act would be

A. *good;* it will help to keep him from doing it again
B. *bad;* it suggests to this subordinate that you have a bad memory
C. *good;* he will know that you have not forgotten an important infraction
D. *bad;* the incident is over and he has not done anything like it since

11. Lately one of the drivers that you supervise has not been doing as good a job as he used to do. He asks whether he may discuss with you a problem that has been bothering him. He says he thinks that the problem has been affecting his work. But after he tells you the problem, you feel that this is really a minor problem and that he has somehow failed to consider certain alternatives open to him.
Of the following, the FIRST thing you should do is to 11.____

A. examine with him possibilities for solving the problem
B. tell him it is a minor problem
C. tell him the solution to the problem
D. explain to him that he must not let such problems disturb him in his work

12. Suppose that you, the dispatcher, instruct a motor vehicle operator to make a delivery and to use a certain route which you believe is the fastest and shortest. The driver then says that he knows a shorter, faster route.
Of the following, it would be BEST for you to 12.____

A. tell the driver to follow your route and not question the orders of his supervisor
B. assign this delivery to a driver who agrees that your route is best
C. ask your supervisor to decide which is the best route so the driver will know that you are open-minded
D. have the driver describe the other route and let him use it if it seems at least as good as yours

13. Your department has just made a major policy change affecting work procedures for the 30 men under your supervision, and they do not yet know about it. You wish to reduce or eliminate lasting negative reactions and to gain as much acceptance of this policy change as possible.
Which of the following is the BEST method to use to accomplish this purpose? 13.____

A. Circulate a memo to them describing the policy change in detail
B. Call a meeting with them to inform them thoroughly of the policy change, and to answer questions
C. Make clear to the men that the policy change was not your idea, but that it must be followed
D. Announce the policy change at a meeting and end the meeting before objections can be raised

14. A driver asks you, the dispatcher, about a suggestion he plans to send in to the employees' suggestion program. You doubt whether his suggestion can be used because you think it will be unacceptable to most employees; that they will resist its use.
Of the following, the BEST thing for you to do would be to tell him 14.____

A. why you do not think he should send in the suggestion
B. your doubts about the suggestion, but encourage him to send it in anyway
C. that you think it is a good suggestion and that he should send it in
D. not to send in the suggestion unless he can think of some way to get employees to accept it

15. A dispatcher should periodically check the procedures and practices in his garage to see whether any changes should be made.
Which of the following is the MAIN reason for checking in this manner? 15.____

A. All necessary changes in procedures can, in this way, be made immediately.
B. Frequent changes in procedures are welcomed by employees.
C. It is the dispatcher's responsibility to try to improve, when possible, the operations he supervises.
D. The dispatcher is fully responsible for deciding the important changes in procedure in his garage.

16. A driver has been transferred from another garage to the one in which you are the dispatcher. The driver's former supervisor calls to tell you that the driver is uncooperative. Of the following, the BEST thing for you to do would be to 16.____

A. tell the driver that you are aware of the fact that he gave very little cooperation to the other dispatcher, but that you will treat him fairly
B. test as soon as possible how much the driver is willing to cooperate
C. wait to see how the driver reacts under your supervision
D. make arrangements to have him transferred to another assignment

17. A driver accuses you, the dispatcher, of favoritism. For you to ask the driver to be more specific would be 17.____

A. *bad;* it may create an argument with consequent bad feelings on both sides
B. *good;* it can help in settling the matter
C. *bad;* it puts the driver in a position where he will have to defend himself
D. *good;* it shows the driver that you are fair

18. Which one of the following is LEAST likely to mean that your drivers like their jobs? 18.____

A. Most of the drivers have excellent attendance reports.
B. The drivers do their work to the best of their ability.
C. The drivers admire and respect their supervisors.
D. Most of the drivers have had at least some high school.

19. Of the following situations, which one would the dispatcher MOST likely be able to handle by himself without discussing it with his superior? 19.____

A. A disagreement comes up between two of his drivers about the meaning of a departmental regulation.
B. Additional drivers are needed because of a permanent increase in the work load.
C. One of the drivers he supervises deliberately disregards his instructions, despite warnings and previous punishment for doing this.
D. The drivers are complaining about the great amount of overtime work required.

20. A dispatcher and a few of his drivers are going to lift a heavy object together. The dispatcher tells the men not to lift until he gives a signal to begin lifting. Of the following, the BEST reason for these instructions is that they help 20.____

A. alert the men to be careful not to hurt themselves when lifting
B. get the men to lift with all their available strength
C. maintain the dispatcher's position as the leader of the group
D. avoid too much strain on any member of the group

KEY (CORRECT ANSWERS)

1.	B	11.	A
2.	C	12.	D
3.	D	13.	B
4.	D	14.	B
5.	A	15.	C
6.	C	16.	C
7.	A	17.	B
8.	B	18.	D
9.	B	19.	A
10.	D	20.	D

TEST 2

DIRECTIONS: Each question or incomplete statement is followed by several suggested answers or completions. Select the one that BEST answers the question or completes the statement. *PRINT THE LETTER OF THE CORRECT ANSWER IN THE SPACE AT THE RIGHT.*

1. The EASIEST and QUICKEST way of finding which spark plug is bad and causing an engine to miss is to 1.____

   A. remove each plug and examine it
   B. replace each plug, one at a time, with a new one
   C. check each plug with a timing light
   D. short circuit each plug, one at a time

2. A pressure cap is used in an automotive cooling system to 2.____

   A. measure the water pressure
   B. prevent cold water from reaching the engine
   C. raise the boiling point of the water
   D. aid circulation of water in the cooling system

3. The necessity to frequently add large amounts of water to a car storage battery is MOST likely an indication that the 3.____

   A. charging rate is too high
   B. charging rate is too low
   C. battery connection is loose
   D. ground connection is loose

4. Inspection of an automobile tire shows that the center treads have had more wear than the side treads. 4.____
   The MOST common cause for this condition is

   A. too much camber
   B. cornering
   C. overinflation
   D. underinflation

5. Graphite is a recommended lubricant for automotive 5.____

   A. springs
   B. car door locks
   C. differentials
   D. steering shafts

6. The ignition coil on a gasoline engine 6.____

   A. transforms low voltage to high voltage
   B. prevents sparking at the breaker points
   C. limits charging voltage on the battery
   D. prevents excessive flow of current to the spark plugs

7. The MAIN function of a thermostat in the radiator of an automobile is to 7.____

   A. prevent cold water from circulating between the engine and the radiator
   B. permit full flow of cooling water to the engine when starting the engine up
   C. prevent cooling water from overheating
   D. alert the driver that the engine is overheating

8. The one of the following automotive components or systems that is NOT considered a part of the *power train* is the 8.____

A. propeller shaft
B. ignition system
C. transmission
D. clutch

9. Suppose in your garage records are kept of the vehicular accidents your men have while driving at work. In addition to the number of accidents each man has, which of the following facts in the records would be the MOST important for comparing drivers on their success in avoiding driving accidents while working? 9.____
The

A. number of years of driving experience of each man
B. number of miles driven by each driver on the job
C. gasoline consumption of each vehicle
D. age of the drivers assigned to the garage

10. A department has asked dispatchers to study the standard forms and reports they fill out each day, and to make recommendations for revision. 10.____
Which of the following is the BEST reason for a dispatcher to suggest that certain information no longer be asked on such forms?

A. The information is no longer applicable to this department.
B. Although the information is accurate, it becomes outdated after a while.
C. The information is difficult to evaluate on the level of the dispatcher.
D. The information requested can only be estimated at ninety-eight percent accuracy.

Questions 11-18.

DIRECTIONS: Questions 11 through 18 are to be answered according to the information given in the notes and map that appear on Page 3 following.

NOTES

A circle with a number inside (③) indicates a street work crew.

A cross (X) indicates an entrance and exit.

Arrows on streets indicate (→) one-way and (↔) two-way streets.

No U-turns are permitted.

Disregard the width of the streets, avenues, and boulevards in arriving at your answers.

Assume that for each standard block shown on the map, the length (from street to street) is twice as big as the width (from avenue to avenue).

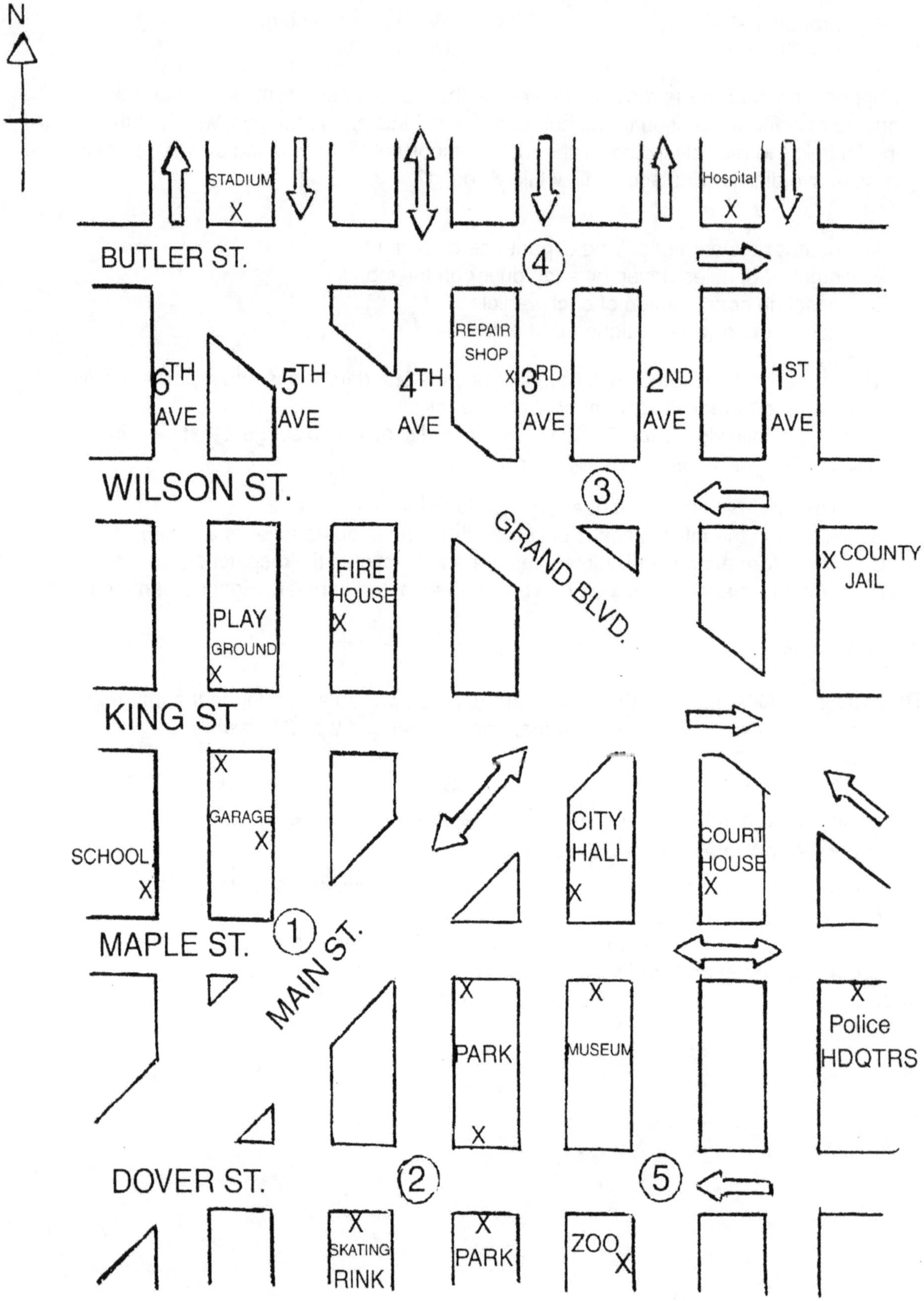
N
STADIUM
X
Hospital
X
BUTLER ST.
4
REPAIR
SHOP
X
6TH
AVE
5TH
AVE
4TH
AVE
3RD
AVE
2ND
AVE
1ST
AVE
WILSON ST.
3
GRAND BLVD.
FIRE
HOUSE
X
PLAY
GROUND
X
X COUNTY
JAIL
KING ST
X
GARAGE
X
SCHOOL
X
CITY
HALL
X
COURT
HOUSE
X
MAPLE ST.
1
MAIN ST.
X
PARK
X
X
MUSEUM
X
Police
HDQTRS
DOVER ST.
2
5
X
SKATING
RINK
X
PARK
ZOO
X

11. A driver should turn left when exiting from the 11.____

A. court house
B. playground
C. stadium
D. repair shop

12. An operator, facing west on Wilson St. and 2nd Ave., wants to drive to Dover St. and 6th Ave. 12.____
The SHORTEST allowable route for him to take is

A. Wilson St., 3rd Ave., and Main St.
B. Wilson St., 5th Ave., and Dover St.
C. Wilson St., 3rd Ave., Maple St., 5th Ave., and Dover St.
D. 2nd Ave., Grand Blvd., and Main St.

13. The SHORTEST allowable route for driving from the repair shop exit to the garage entrance is to use Third Ave., 13.____

A. Maple St., and 6th Ave.
B. and King St.
C. Main St., and 5th Ave.
D. Wilson St., and 5th Ave.

14. An emergency repair has to be made in front of the entrance to the fire house and a work crew is needed there immediately. The dispatcher is told to send the crew that can reach the fire house entrance first, using the shortest allowable driving distance. 14.____
Which crew should he send?
Crew

A. 1
B. 2
C. 3
D. 4

15. Which describes BEST the location of the museum in relation to the school? 15.____
The museum is located ______ of the school.

A. southwest
B. southeast
C. northwest
D. northeast

16. Work Crew 5 will be finished with its job at 1 P.M. and has to join Work Crew 3 for the rest of the day. Work Crew 4 will also be finished at 1 P.M. and must join Work Crew 2 for the rest of the day. The driver of the truck is to start from inside the garage, take Work Crews 5 and 4 to their new locations, and return into the garage. Of the following choices, the driver will cover the SHORTEST allowable route if he picks up crew 16.____

A. 5, drops off crew 5 at crew 3, picks up crew 4, drops off crew 4 at crew 2
B. 4, picks up crew 5, drops off crew 5 at crew 3, drops off crew 4 at crew 2
C. 4, drops off crew 4 at crew 2, picks up crew 5, drops off crew 5 at crew 3
D. 5, picks up crew 4, drops off crew 5 at crew 3, drops off crew 4 at crew 2

17. One operator is assigned to pick up a city official at the hospital and drive him to the entrance to City Hall. The SHORTEST allowable route to take from the hospital is Butler St., First Ave., 17.____

A. Maple St., and Third Ave.
B. Wilson St. 2nd Ave., Grand Blvd., Main St., and Third Ave.
C. Maple St., Main St., and Third Ave.
D. Wilson St., and Third Ave.

18. Of the following, which entrance is the SHORTEST allowable driving distance from the school exit? 18.____
The entrance to

A. the hospital
B. police headquarters
C. the County Jail
D. the museum

Questions 19-20.

DIRECTIONS: A city vehicle has been involved in an accident and a diagram of the accident has been prepared. Answer Questions 19 and 20 according to the information given in the diagram and notes below.

Diagram of An Accident

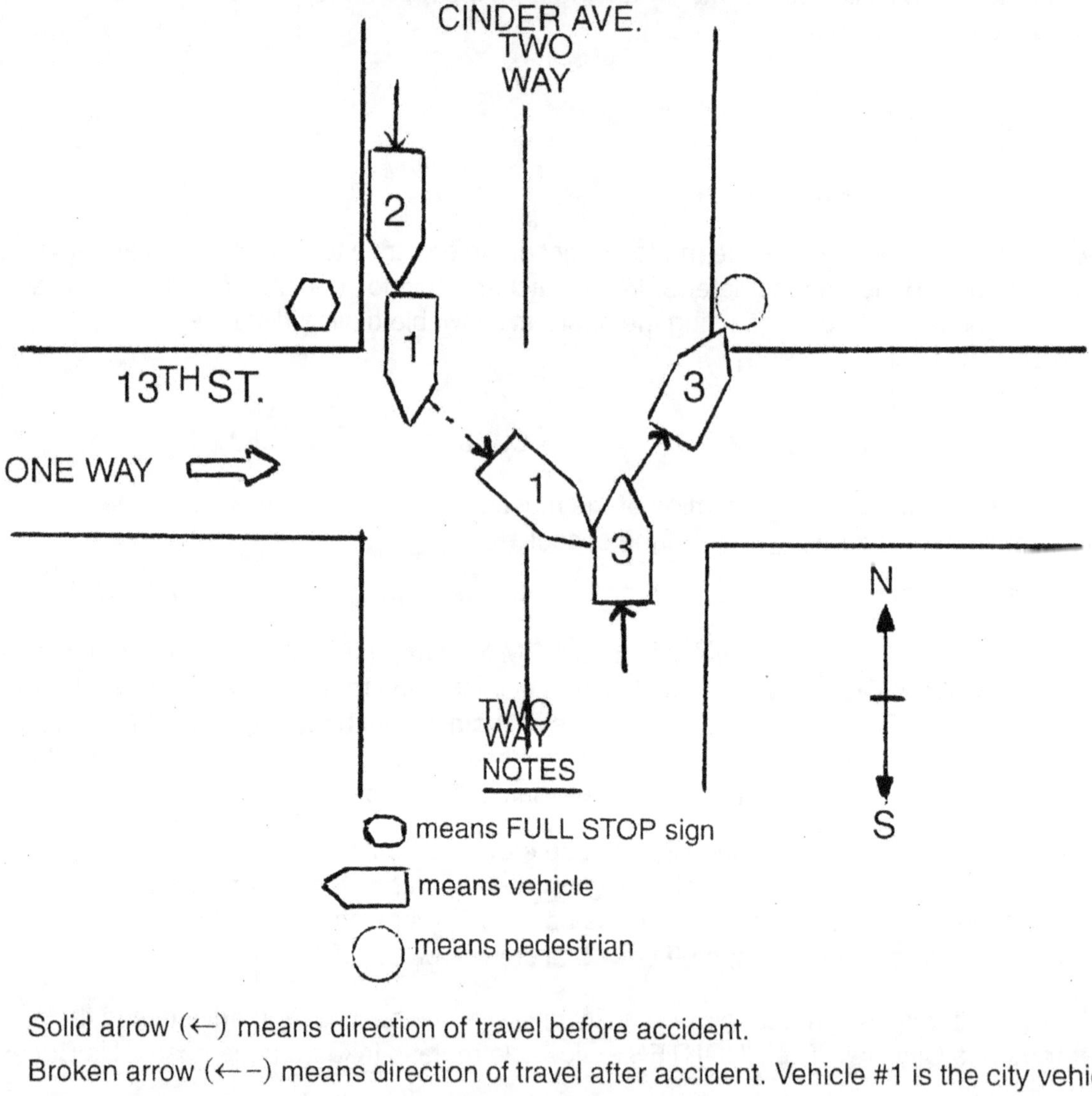

Solid arrow (←) means direction of travel before accident.
Broken arrow (←--) means direction of travel after accident. Vehicle #1 is the city vehicle.

19. The FULL STOP sign is located on the ______ corner of the intersection. 19.____

A. northeast B. northwest C. southeast D. southwest

20. If the driver of the city vehicle was following driving regulations, it is MOST likely that at the time he was hit he was 20.____

   A. making a right turn
   B. making a left turn
   C. standing still
   D. driving down Cinder Avenue

KEY (CORRECT ANSWERS)

1.	D	11.	C
2.	C	12.	A
3.	A	13.	D
4.	C	14.	C
5.	B	15.	B
6.	A	16.	A
7.	A	17.	D
8.	B	18.	D
9.	B	19.	B
10.	A	20.	D

TEST 3

DIRECTIONS: Each question or incomplete statement is followed by several suggested answers or completions. Select the one that BEST answers the question or completes the statement. *PRINT THE LETTER OF THE CORRECT ANSWER IN THE SPACE AT THE RIGHT.*

Questions 1-19.

DIRECTIONS: In each of Questions 1 through 19, choose the lettered word which means MOST NEARLY the same as the word in capital letters.

1. APPRAISE 1.____
   A. inform B. evaluate C. increase D. decrease

2. IMPARTIAL 2.____
   A. strange B. funny C. fair D. bad

3. INCENTIVE 3.____
   A. cash B. fire C. messenger D. motive

4. INSUBORDINATE 4.____
   A. confusing B. disobedient C. important D. smart

5. NEGLIGENT 5.____
   A. careless B. painful C. cruel D. untidy

6. REVISION 6.____
   A. change B. decision C. dream D. retreat

7. SEMIANNUALLY 7.____
   A. four times in a year B. three times in a year C. twice in a year D. every other year

8. UTILIZE 8.____
   A. break B. cook C. reduce D. use

9. VAGUE 9.____
   A. new B. sure C. old D. uncertain

10. CENTRIFUGAL 10.____
    A. moving away from a center
    B. moving toward a center
    C. having a center
    D. without a center

11. INDUCE 11.____

A. cause B. stop C. name D. signal

12. PERTINENT 12.____

A. wise
B. stormy
C. relevant
D. understood

13. ENUMERATE 13.____

A. free B. count C. postpone D. obey

14. DEPLETE 14.____

A. hide B. order C. purchase D. empty

15. DIVERSE 15.____

A. average B. varied C. faulty D. hollow

16. MESH 16.____

A. engage B. skip C. spin D. use

17. DISMANTLE 17.____

A. lock up
B. forget about
C. look over
D. take apart

18. INCIDENTAL 18.____

A. casual
B. necessary
C. infrequent
D. needless

19. ELASTIC 19.____

A. resilient
B. reserved
C. tranquil
D. sterile

20. Truck A has been driven 38,742.3 miles, Truck B has been driven 24,169.7 miles, Truck C has been driven 41,286.4 miles, Truck D has been driven 15,053.5 miles, and Truck E has been driven 8,407.0 miles. 20.____
The total mileage of these five trucks combined is MOST NEARLY _____ miles.

A. 127,650 B. 127,660 C. 128,650 D. 128,660

21. Suppose that the trucks in a certain garage used a total of 86,314 gallons of gas in 1991 and 8,732 gallons less in 1992. 21.____
If they used a total of 72,483 gallons of gas in 1993, how much LESS gas was used in 1993 than in 1992?
_______ gallons.

A. 5,099 B. 5,109 C. 5,199 D. 5,209

22. A driver averaged 17 miles for each gallon of gas used one week and 26 miles the next week. 22.____
If he used 38.9 gallons during the first week and 27.6 during the second, the TOTAL number of miles he drove in these two weeks was ______ miles.

A. 1,266.3 B. 1,322.6 C. 1,378.9 D. 1,435.2

23. In Garage A, 87 drivers worked a total of 427 hours overtime. In Garage B, 53 drivers worked a total of 245 hours overtime. 23.____
Compared to the average overtime worked per man in Garage B, the average overtime worked per man in Garage A was MOST NEARLY ______ of an hour ______.

A. 2/10; more
B. 2/10; less
C. 3/10; more
D. 3/10; less

24. The scale on a map indicates that every 1 5/8 inches on the map represents 5 miles. 24.____
If two locations are 13 inches apart on the map, what is the distance between them, in miles?

A. 30 B. 35 C. 40 D. 45

25. If a car is traveling on a highway at a steady speed of 35 miles an hour, how many miles will it go in a period of 24 minutes? 25.____
______ miles.

A. 13 B. 14 C. 15 D. 16

26. An employee's annual salary is $7,625. 26.____
If he receives a 5.4% salary increase, his new annual salary will be

A. $7,992.50
B. $8,036.75
C. $8,147.25
D. $8,169.00

27. Of the 60 drivers assigned to a garage, 1/6 of them live in County A, 1/4 of them live in County B, 1/5 of them live in County C, and the rest live in County D. 27.____
How many of the drivers live in County D?

A. 22 B. 23 C. 24 D. 25

28. Driver Green travels 33 miles along express highways at an average speed of 44 miles an hour to get to his destination. Driver Smith travels 28 miles through traffic at an average speed of 21 miles an hour to get to the same destination. 28.____
If Mr. Smith starts his trip a half hour before Mr. Green, he will reach the destination ______ Mr. Green.

A. 5 minutes before
B. at the same time as
C. 5 minutes after
D. 10 minutes after

29. A 210 foot by 120 foot parking lot is reduced in size by construction of a 36 foot by 54 foot building at one of its corners. 29.____
The area left for parking is MOST NEARLY ______ square yards.

A. 1,800 B. 2,600 C. 22,800 D. 23,300

30. A dispatcher works a total of 44 hours, spending 17 on Special Project A, 13 on Special Project B, and the rest on his usual duties. 30.____
The percentage of time he spends on the two special projects is MOST NEARLY

A. 68% B. 69% C. 70% D. 71%

31. A driver, dispatched from the garage at 8:15 A.M., arrived at his first destination 35 minutes later. He waited 50 minutes at this location before he could go on to his next destination. It took him one hour and 40 minutes traveling time to get to this second location. He then took an hour lunch period before driving back to the garage, a trip that took 45 minutes. 31.____
What time did the driver return to the garage?
______ P.M.

A. 12:25 B. 12:45 C. 1:05 D. 1:25

Questions 32-35.

DIRECTIONS: Questions 32 through 35 are to be answered according to the information given in the following passage.

<u>*ACCIDENT PRONENESS*</u>

Accident proneness is a subject deserving much more attention than it has received. Studies have shown a high incidence of accidents to be associated with particular employees who are called accident prone. Such employees, according to these studies, behave on their jobs in ways which make them likely to have more accidents than would normally be expected.

It is important to point out the difference between the employee who is a "repeater" and the one who is truly accident prone. It is obvious that any person assigned to work about which he knows little will be liable to injury until he does learn the "how" of the job. Few workers left completely on their own will develop adequate safe practices. Therefore, they must be trained. Only those who fail to respond to proper training should be regarded as accident prone.

The dangers of an occupation should also be considered when judging an accident record. For a crane operator, a record of five accidents in a given period of time may not indicate accident proneness, while, in the case of a clerk, two accidents over the same period of time may be excessive. There are the repeaters whose accident records can be explained by correctible physical defects, by correctible unsafe plant or machine conditions, or by assignment to work for which they are not suited because they cannot meet all the job's physical requirements. Such repeaters cannot be fairly called "accident prone." A diagnosis of accident proneness should not be lightly made, but should be based on all of these considerations .

32. According to the above passage, studies have shown that accident prone employees 32.____

A. work under unsafe physical conditions
B. act in unsafe ways on the job
C. are not usually physically suited for their jobs
D. work in the more dangerous occupations

33. According to the above passage, a person who is accident prone 33.____

A. has received proper training which has not reduced his tendency toward accidents
B. repeats the same accident several times over a short period of time
C. experiences excessive anxiety about dangers in his occupation
D. ignores unsafe but correctible machine conditions

34. According to the above passage, MOST persons who are given work they know little about 34.___

A. will eventually learn on their own sufficient safety practices to follow
B. work safely if they are not accident prone
C. must be trained before they develop adequate safety methods
D. should be regarded as accident prone until they become familiar with the job

35. According to the above passage, to effectively judge the accident record of an employee, one should consider 35.___

A. the employee's age and physical condition
B. that five accidents are excessive
C. the type of dangers that are natural to his job
D. the difficulty level of previous occupations held by the employee

Questions 36-39.

DIRECTIONS: Questions 36 through 39 are to be answered according to the information given in the following paragraph.

FIRES

The four types of fives are called Class A, Class B, Class C, and Class D. Examples of Class A fires are paper, cloth, or wood fires. The types of extinguishers used on Class A fires are foam, soda acid, or water. Class B fires are those in burning liquids. They require a smothering action for extinguishment. Carbon dioxide, dry chemical, vaporizing liquid, or foam are the types of extinguishers that are used on burning liquids. Electrical fires, such as in motors and switches, are Class C fires. A non-conducting extinguishing agent must be used for this kind of fire. Therefore, carbon dioxide, dry chemical, or vaporizing liquid extinguishers are used. Fires in motor vehicles are Class D fires, and carbon dioxide, dry chemical, or vaporizing liquid extinguishers should be used on them.

36. According to the information in the above paragraph, a fire in a can full of gasoline would be a Class _______ fire. 36.___

A. D B. C C. B D. A

37. In the above paragraph, the extinguishers recommended are entirely the same for Class _______ and Class _______ fires. 37.___

A. B; D B. C; D C. B; C D. A; B

38. According to the information in the above paragraph, a water extinguisher would MOST likely be suitable for use on which one of the following fires? 38.___
A(n)

A. fire in a truck engine
B. fire in an electrical switch
C. oil fire
D. lumber fire

39. According to the information in the above paragraph, dry chemical 39.____

A. should not be used on a burning liquid fire
B. is a conducting extinguishing agent
C. should not be used on a fire in a car
D. smothers fires to put them out

Questions 40-45.

DIRECTIONS: The table below shows the initial requests made by staff for vacation. It is to be used with the Rules and Guidelines to make the decisions and judgments called for in each of Questions 40 through 45.

VACATION REQUESTS FOR THE ONE YEAR PERIOD
FROM
MAY 1, YEAR X, THROUGH APRIL 30, YEAR Y

NAME	WORK ASSIGNMENT	DATE APPOINTED	ACCUMULATED ANNUAL LEAVE DAYS	VACATION PERIODS REQUESTED
DeMarco	MVO	Mar. 2003	25	May 3-21; Oct. 25-Nov. 5
Moore	Dispatcher	Dec. 1997	32	May 24-June 4; July 12-16
Kingston	MVO	Apr. 2007	28	May 24-June 11; Feb. 7-25
Green	MVO	June 2006	26	June 7-18; Sept. 6-24
Robinson	MVO	July 1998	30	June 28-July 9; Nov. 15-26
Reilly	MVO	Oct. 2009	23	July 5-9; Jan. 31-Mar. 3
Stevens	MVO	Sept. 1996	31	July 5-23; Oct. 4-29
Costello	MVO	Sept. 1998	31	July 5-30; Oct. 4-22
Maloney	Dispatcher	Aug. 1992	35	July 5-Aug. 6; Nov. 1-5
Hughes	Director	Feb. 1990	38	July 26-Sept. 3
Lord	MVO	Jan. 2010	20	Aug. 9-27; Feb. 7-25
Diaz	MVO	Dec. 2009	28	Aug. 9-Sept. 10
Krimsky	MVO	May 2006	22	Oct. 18-22; Nov. 22-Dec. 10

RULES AND GUIDELINES

1. The two dispatchers cannot be on vacation at the same time, nor can a dispatcher be on vacation at the same time as the director.

2. For the period June 1 through September 30, not more than three MVO's can be on vacation at the same time.

3. For the period October 1 through May 31, not more than two MVO's at a time can be on vacation.

4. In cases where the same vacation time is requested by too many employees for all of them to be given the time under the rules, the requests of those who have worked the longest will be granted.

5. No employee may take more leave days than the number of annual leave days accumulated and shown in the table.

6. All vacation periods shown in the table and described in the questions below begin on a Monday and end on a Friday.

7. Employees work a five day week (Monday through Friday). They are off weekends and holidays with no charges to leave balances. When a holiday falls on a Saturday or Sunday, employees are given the following Mondav off without charge to annual leave.

8. Holidays:

May 31	October 25	January 1
July 4	November 2	February 12
September 6	November 25	February 21
October 11	December 25	

9. An employee shall be given any part of his initial requests that is permissible under the above rules and shall have first right to it despite any further adjustment of schedule.

40. Until adjustments in the vacation schedule can be made, the vacation dates that can be approved for Krimsky are 40.____

A. Oct. 18-22; Nov. 22-Dec. 10
B. Oct. 18-22; Nov. 29-Dec. 10
C. Oct. 18-22 only
D. Nov. 22-Dec. 10 only

41. Until adjustments in the vacation schedule can be made, the vacation dates that can be approved for Maloney are 41.____

A. July 5-Aug. 6; Nov. 1-5
B. July 5-23; Nov. 1-5
C. July 5-9; Nov. 1-5
D. Nov. 1-5 only

42. According to the table, Lord wants a vacation in August and another in February. Until adjustments in the vacation schedule can be made, he can be allowed to take _______ of the August vacation _______ of the February vacation. 42.____

A. all; but none
B. all; and almost half
C. almost all; and almost half
D. almost half; and all

43. Costello cannot be given all the vacation he has requested because 43.____

A. the MVO's who have more seniority than he has have requested time he wishes
B. he does not have enough accumulated annual leave
C. a dispatcher is applying for vacation at the same time as Costello
D. there are five people who want vacation in July

44. According to the table, how many leave days will DeMarco be charged for his vacation from October 25 through November 5? 44.____

A. 10 B. 9 C. 8 D. 7

45. How many leave days will Moore use if he uses the requested vacation allowable to him under the rules? 45.____

A. 9 B. 10 C. 14 D. 15

KEY (CORRECT ANSWERS)

1.	B	11.	A	21.	A	31.	C	41.	B
2.	C	12.	C	22.	C	32.	B	42.	A
3.	D	13.	B	23.	C	33.	A	43.	B
4.	B	14.	D	24.	C	34.	C	44.	C
5.	A	15.	B	25.	B	35.	C	45.	A
6.	A	16.	A	26.	B	36.	C		
7.	C	17.	D	27.	B	37.	B		
8.	D	18.	A	28.	C	38.	D		
9.	D	19.	A	29.	B	39.	D		
10.	A	20.	B	30.	A	40.	D		

EXAMINATION SECTION

TEST 1

DIRECTIONS: Each question or incomplete statement is followed by several suggested answers or completions. Select the one that BEST answers the question or completes the statement. *PRINT THE LETTER OF THE CORRECT ANSWER IN THE SPACE AT THE RIGHT.*

1. Front stabilizer bars on automotive vehicles are set in such a manner that they 1.____
   A. apply force opposite to that of the springs when the springs are deflected equally
   B. normally connect to both lower control arms
   C. are adjustable in order to level the vehicle
   D. have one end attached to the lower control arm and the other end attached to the frame

2. Ignition point contact alignment is BEST adjusted by bending the 2.____
   A. movable point arm
   B. pivot post
   C. breaker plate
   D. stationary point bracket

3. When disc brakes are retracted so as not to be touching the braking disc, the amount of retraction 3.____
   A. is affected by the piston return springs
   B. must be a minimum of 1/32 of an inch
   C. is affected by the piston seals
   D. is limited by the metering valve

4. A PROPERLY operating positive crankcase ventilation valve will 4.____
   A. control air flow as a direct function of engine speed
   B. increase air flow in direct proportion to the increase in manifold vacuum
   C. shut off air flow at high intake manifold vacuum
   D. reduce air flow at high intake manifold vacuum

5. The air-fuel ratio, by weight, in a properly functioning gasoline automotive engine is MOST NEARLY 5.____
   A. 15:1
   B. 30:1
   C. 600:1
   D. 9000:1

6. Cam ground pistons are distinguished by 6.____
   A. being ground perfectly round
   B. having a larger diameter across the piston pin faces
   C. having a larger diameter parallel to the crankshaft centerline
   D. having a larger diameter perpendicular to the crankshaft centerline

7. In an automotive engine, the intake valves USUALLY open _____ TDC and close _____ BDC of the intake stroke. 7.____
   A. after; after
   B. after; before
   C. before; before
   D. before; after

8. In an automotive engine, the exhaust valves USUALLY open _____ BDC of the power stroke and _____ TDC of the intake stroke. 8.____
   A. after; before
   B. before; before
   C. before; after
   D. after; after

9. The PRIMARY function of a blower on a two-cycle diesel engine is to 9.____
   A. provide air for scavenging
   B. increase the compression ratio
   C. blow in the fuel-air mixture
   D. cool the oil after compression in the injector pump

10. Excessive free travel of the clutch pedal would be indicated if the 10.____
   A. transmission was hard to shift smoothly
   B. clutch slipped when fully engaged
   C. throwout bearing failed prematurely
   D. release levers were worn

11. Vacuum is usually referred to in inches of mercury. 11.____
   The number of pounds per square inch pressure above zero (absolute pressure) of a 20 inch vacuum is MOST NEARLY
   A. 4.9
   B. 7.4
   C. 9.6
   D. 11.8

12. Only a portion of the heat energy released by the gasoline in an automotive engine is transmitted to the wheels for driving purposes. 12.____
   In an automobile in good condition and with an efficiently operating engine, this portion is MOST NEARLY
   A. 90%
   B. 50%
   C. 20%
   D. 2%

13. An adjustment is made to the right front wheel of a vehicle equipped with shims at the junction of the upper suspension arm and the frame support by moving the upper suspension arm away from the frame a greater amount in the front than in the rear. This is done to 13.____
   A. increase the steering knuckle angle
   B. adjust the caster in a negative direction
   C. adjust the camber in a negative direction
   D. adjust the caster in a rotary direction

14. In an automotive rear axle in which the pinion gear engages the ring gear below the centerline of the axle, the cut of the pinion and ring gear is 14.____
   A. spiral bevel
   B. spur bevel
   C. double helical
   D. hypoid

15. Of the following statements concerning the operation in low gear of a fully synchronized (in forward gears) three-speed transmission, the one that is NOT correct is that 15.____
   A. both clutch sleeves must engage gears
   B. power is being transmitted through the countershaft gears
   C. one clutch sleeve must be engaged
   D. the reverse idler gear is being driven by a countershaft gear

Questions 16-17.

DIRECTIONS: Questions 16 and 17 are to be answered in accordance with the following paragraph.

Steam cleaners get their name from the fact that steam is used to generate pressure and is also a by-product of heating the cleaning solution. Steam itself as little cleaning power. It will melt some soils, but it does not dissolve them, break them up, or destroy their clinging power. Rather surprisingly, good machines generate as little steam as possible. Modern surface chemistry depends on a chemical solution to dissolve dirt, destroy its clinging power, and hold it in suspension. Steam actually hinders such a solution, but heat helps its physical and chemical action. Cleaning is most efficient when a hot solution reaches the work in heavy volume.

16. In accordance with the above paragraph, for MOST efficient cleaning, 16.____
    A. a heavy volume of steam is needed
    B. hot steam is needed to break up the soils
    C. steam is used to dissolve the surface dirt
    D. a hot chemical solution should always be used

17. When reference to the above paragraph, the steam in a steam cleaner is used to 17.____
    A. generate pressure
    B. create by-product chemicals
    C. slow down the chemical action of the cleaning solution
    D. dissolve accumulations of dirt

18. An electromechanical regulator for an automotive alternator differs from a DC generator in that the alternator regulator 18.____
    A. has a current regulator unit
    B. has a reverse current relay
    C. does not have a current regulator unit
    D. does not have a voltage regulator unit

19. Of the following statements concerning the charging of lead acid batteries, the one MOST NEARLY correct is that 19.____
    A. a fast charge (40-50 amp, 2V) can safely be used if the battery temperature does not exceed 185° F
    B. heavily sulphated batteries respond best to a slow charging rate
    C. a battery on trickle charge cannot be damaged by overcharging
    D. the higher the battery temperature, the smaller the charging current with constant applied voltage

20. The ignition points of a conventional ignition system are adjusted to increase the point gap. 20.____
    This adjustment will
    A. increase the dwell angle
    B. retard the ignition timing
    C. advance the ignition timing
    D. decrease the dwell angle with no change in ignition timing

21. A single diaphragm distributor vacuum advance unit 21.____
    A. advances the spark under part throttle operation
    B. is connected to the intake manifold
    C. advances the spark in proportion to engine speed
    D. advances the spark during acceleration or full throttle operation

22. The part of a conventional ignition system that could properly be considered part of BOTH the primary and secondary circuits would be the 22.____
    A. condenser
    B. distributor rotor
    C. coil
    D. ignition points

23. As compared to a conventional type of spark plug, a resistor type of spark plug will 23.____
    A. reduce the inductive portion of the spark
    B. lengthen the capacitive portion of the spark
    C. require a higher voltage to function properly
    D. have an auxiliary air gap

24. If the criterion that limits the yearly major repair expenses to 30% of the current value of equipment were reduced to 15% and the depreciation rate of 20% of original cost each year were increased to 25%, the expenses for major repairs in a shop handling a constant flow of equipment of the same type and age would 24.____
    A. increase slightly
    B. remain the same
    C. increase slightly
    D. increase markedly

Question 25.

DIRECTIONS: Question 25 is to be answered in accordance with the following paragraph.

The storage battery is a lead-acid, electrochemical device used for storing energy in its chemical form. The battery does not actually store electricity, but converts an electrical charge into chemical energy which is stored until the battery terminals are connected to a closed external circuit. When the circuit is closed, the chemical energy inside the battery is transformed back into electrical energy through a chemical action, and, as a result, current flows through the circuit.

25. According to the above paragraph, a lead-acid battery stores 25.____
    A. current
    B. electricity
    C. electrical energy
    D. chemical energy

26. A cam is to be fashioned from a circular disc with a hole drilled eccentrically on a diameter of the disc but perpendicularly to the surface of the disc. A keyed shaft is to be fitted into the hole so that the disc may be rotated in order to function as a cam. If the disc is 5 inches in diameter and ½ inch thick and the hole is to be 1 inch in diameter, the distance from the center of the disc to the center of the hole to be drilled in order for the disc to act as a cam with a 2 inch lift should be _____ inch(es). 26.____
    A. 2
    B. 1½
    C. 1
    D. ½

27. Sparks and open flames should be kept away from batteries that are being charged because of the danger of explosion or fire resulting from the ignition of the generated _____ gas. 27.____
    A. fluorine B. nitrogen C. hydrogen D. argon

28. Safety standards indicate that the use of any motor vehicle equipment having an obstructed view to the rear 28.____
    A. requires a reverse signal alarm audible above the surrounding noise level
    B. requires the use of two back-up lights of at least 45 watt capacity each
    C. requires the use of a safety contact alarm rear bumper audible above the surrounding noise level
    D. is prohibited

29. In the performance of a compression test, it is found that the addition of a tablespoon of SAE 40 motor oil causes no significant increase in the low compression pressure. 29.____
    The low compression pressure is most probably NOT caused by
    A. a broken piston B. a leaking head gasket
    C. sticking valves D. worn piston rings

30. Automotive exhaust gas analyzers, as generally used in emission control maintenance, will normally indicate the percentage of 30.____
    A.NO B. SO_2 C. CO_2 D. CO

Questions 31-33.

DIRECTIONS: Questions 31 through 33 are to be answered in accordance with the information given below.

For most efficient utilization of funds and facilities, the rule has been established that the repair cost of a part cannot exceed 50% of the vendor's price for a new part and that a part cannot be made in-house if the cost would be more than 70% of the vendor's price for a new one.

You have found that the average removed sprocket shaft, as shown below, requires both bearing sections to be built up and remachined and one sprocket section to be built up and remachined. The foreman of the machine shop has given you the following information relative to the manufacture or repair of the shafts:

	Time	Rate
Weld 1 bearing section	1.2 hours	$40/hr.
Weld 1 keyway and sprocket section	2.0 hours	$40/hr.
Turn 1 bearing section	0.6 hours	$40/hr.
Turn 1 sprocket section	0.7 hours	$40/hr.
Cut 1 keyway	0.5 hours	$40/hr.

Purchasing has quoted shaft material at $60/ft. and new shafts at $800 each.

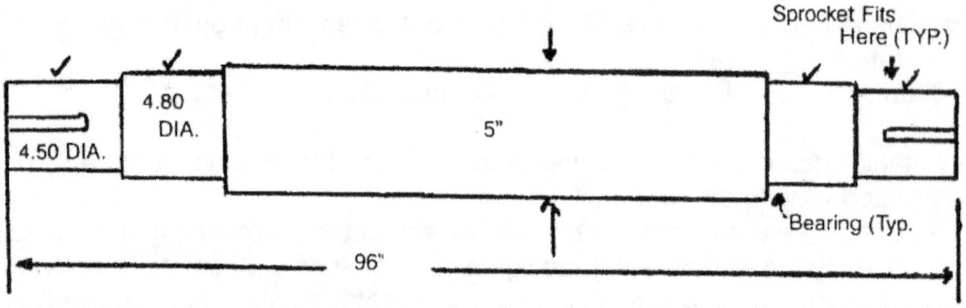

31. In accordance with the information given above, the cost for in-house manufacture of one shaft is 31.____
    A. $552.00 B. $560.00 C. $624.00 D. $663.00

32. In accordance with the information given above, the cost of in-house repair of one shaft is 32.____
    A. $342.00 B. $272.00 C. $152.00 D. $72.00

33. In accordance with the information given above, the PROPER procedure to follow, under the given rules, is to 33.____
    A. repair old shafts and buy new shafts
    B. repair old shafts and make new shafts
    C. make no repairs but make new shafts
    D. make no repairs but buy new shafts

34. The series of small vertical oscillations in the area of the center of a superimposed pattern on the screen of a properly adjusted oscilloscope showing the secondary circuit of a properly tuned automotive engine directly follows the instant at which the 34.____
    A. spark plugs fire B. points open
    C. points close D. coil starts to discharge

35. A rectangularly shaped repair facility for light trucks is 160 feet wide and 260 feet long. A 10 foot space is provided along each wall for benches and equipment. A 60 foot wide area in the middle of the floor is to remain clear for its entire 260 foot length. The entrance to the shop is at one end of this open area. 35.____
    Assuming that there are no columns to contend with, the MAXIMUM area available for parking of trucks is _____ square feet.
    A. 15,600 B. 19,200 C. 26,000 D. 42,600

36. A criterion is established that limits the early major repair expenses to 30% of the current value of the equipment. Equipment is depreciated at a rate of 20% of its original cost each year. A truck purchased on January 1, 2020 for $9,000 had a reconditioned engine installed in February 2023 at a total cost of $900. The amount of money available for additional major repairs on this truck in 2023 was 36.____
    A. none B. $180 C. $360 D. $720

37. Twenty fuel injectors are ordered for your shop by the purchasing department. The terms are list, less 30%, less 10%, less 5%.
If the list price of a fuel injector is $70 and all terms ae met upon delivery, the charges to your budget will be 37.____
A. $1,359.60 B. $1,085.40 C. $837.90 D. $630.80

38. The cylinders of an 8 cylinder automotive engine have a bore of 4 inches and the pistons have a stroke of 4 inches.
If the clearance volume in each cylinder is 6.0 cubic inches, the cubic inch displacement of the engine is MOST NEARLY 38.____
A. 306 B. 354 C. 402 D. 450

39. An automotive engine cylinder has a bore of 4 inches and its pistons have a stroke of 4 inches.
If the clearance volume in the cylinder is 6.0 cubic inches, the compression ratio is MOST NEARLY 39.____
A. 10.62:1 B. 9.37:1 C. 8.37:1 D. 7.62:1

40. Of the following deficiencies found during the inspection of passenger car brakes for issuance of a State Certificate of Inspection, the one that would be cause for REJECTION of the car brakes is that 40.____
A. there is less than 3/64 in. of lining remaining above the drum brake shoe lining rivet heads
B. the master cylinder brake fluid level is anything less than full
C. the brake drums have been found to be more than .020 inches oversize
D. the brake pedal reserve is less than one-half the total possible travel

41. When checking a fuel pump for proper operation, it is ALWAYS necessary to 41.____
A. connect a vacuum gage to the fuel line between the pump and the carburetor
B. make the vacuum test before the pressure test
C. set the gages at floor level to maintain a consistent reference point
D. make a vacuum test if the pressure or volume test results are not up to specification

42. On a single cylinder 4 stroke cycle internal combustion engine equipped with a flywheel magneto, the ignition points open at the end of the ______ strokes. 42.____
A. intake and the compression B. compression and the exhaust
C. power and the compression D. intake and the power

43. An impulse coupling is MOST usually found in 43.____
A. an automatic transmission
B. a limited slip differential
C. the front axle of 4 wheel drive vehicles
D. a magneto

Questions 44-45.

DIRECTIONS: Questions 44 and 45 are to be answered in accordance with the following paragraph.

You have been instructed to expedite the fabrication of four special salt spreader trucks using chassis that are available in the shop. All four trucks must be delivered before the opening of business on December 1, 2021. Based on workload and available hours, the foreman of the body shop indicates that he could manufacture one complete salt spreader body in five weeks, with one additional week required for mounting and securing each body to the available chassis. No work could begin on the body until the engines and hydraulic components, which would have to be purchased, were available for use. The purchasing department has promised delivery of engines and hydraulic components three months after the order is placed. (Assume that all months have four weeks and the same crew is doing the assembling and manufacturing.)

44. With reference to the above paragraph, assuming that the purchasing department placed the order at the beginning of the first week in February 2020 and ultimate delivery of the firs salt spreader truck would be CLOSEST to the end of the _____ week in _____, 2021. 44.____
   A. fourth; July
   B. second; August
   C. fourth; August
   D. first; September

45. With reference to the above paragraph, the LATEST date that the engines and associated hydraulic components could be requisitioned in order to meet the specified deadline would be CLOSEST to the beginning of the _____ week in _____, 2021. 45.____
   A. first; February
   B. first; March
   C. third; March
   D. first; April

46. In an OHV internal combustion engine, excessive inlet valve guide clearance manifests itself initially by 46.____
   A. lowered cylinder compression pressure
   B. excessive oil consumption
   C. increased manifold vacuum
   D. fluffy black deposits on spark plugs

47. One of your mechanics has performed an automotive fuel system test and reports a fuel flow of ½ pint/minute at 500 rpm, a static fuel pump discharge pressure of 6 psi, and a 15 in.Hg vacuum at the pump inlet flex line. These results should suggest to the mechanic that 47.____
   A. the system was operating properly
   B. he should check for a leaking pump inlet flex line
   C. he should replace the defective fuel pump
   D. check for a plugged inlet fuel line

48. An electrician is wiring a light switch on a light truck. The light switch will operate the following lamp bulbs: 48.____

Quantity	No.	Description	Current (Each)
2	194	Marker	.3
3	67	Clearance	.4
2	1157	Stop/Tail	2.1/.6
2	1141	Front Park	1.5
2	6012	Headlamp	4.2/3.4

The parking lamps are to be on when the headlamps are on.
If the permissible current capacities of wire are

16 gage	0 – 6 amp
14 gage	6 – 15 amp
12 gage	15 – 20 amp
10 gage	20 – 25 amp,

the smallest size wire that the electrician should use to supply power to the switch would be a _____ gage wire.
A. 16 B. 14 C. 12 D. 10

49. In an automotive cooling system, the bypass passage or bypass valve 49.____
A. permits a small amount of coolant to pass around the thermostat to maintain circulation
B. permits the circulation of coolant through the engine block when the thermostat is closed
C. directly connects the pump inlet to the pump discharge to prevent cavitation in the pump
D. prevents the coolant in the system from developing excessive pressure

50. When adjusting a recirculating ball worm-and-nut steering gear, it is IMPROPER procedure to 50.____
A. remove the pitman arm before making adjustments
B. loosen the lash adjustment before checking bearing preload
C. make the pitman shaft gear over center adjustment with the steering wheel in the center of travel position
D. adjust the bearing preload with the steering wheel in the center of travel position

KEY (CORRECT ANSWERS)

1.	B	11.	A	21.	A	31.	C	41.	D
2.	D	12.	C	22.	C	32.	B	42.	B
3.	C	13.	B	23.	A	33.	A	43.	D
4.	D	14.	D	24.	A	34.	C	44.	A
5.	A	15.	A	25.	D	35.	B	45.	B
6.	D	16.	D	26.	C	36.	B	46.	B
7.	D	17.	A	27.	C	37.	C	47.	D
8.	C	18.	C	28.	A	38.	C	48.	B
9.	A	19.	B	29.	D	39.	B	49.	B
10.	A	20.	C	30.	D	40.	B	50.	D

EXAMINATION SECTION
TEST 1

DIRECTIONS: Each question or incomplete statement is followed by several suggested answers or completions. Select the one that BEST answers the question or completes the statement. *PRINT THE LETTER OF THE CORRECT ANSWER IN THE SPACE AT THE RIGHT.*

1. Of the following, the one that is a grease fitting is a ______ fitting. 1.____

   A. Morse
   B. Brown and Sharpe
   C. Zerk
   D. caliper

2. In an automobile equipped with an ammeter, the ammeter is used to 2.____

   A. indicate current flow
   B. regulate current flow
   C. act as a circuit breaker
   D. measure engine r.p.m.

3. The ignition points in the distributor of a gasoline engine are opened by means of a 3.____

   A. spring
   B. vacuum
   C. cam with lobes
   D. gear

4. MOST automobile engines that use gasoline as fuel operate as ______ engines. 4.____

   A. single cycle
   B. single stroke, single cycle
   C. two-stroke, two-cycle
   D. four-stroke, two-cycle

5. For a shop manager, the MOST important reason that equipment which is used infrequently should be considered for disposal is that 5.____

   A. such equipment may cause higher management to think that your shop is not busy
   B. the time required for its maintenance could be better used elsewhere
   C. the men may resent having to work on such equipment
   D. such equipment usually has a higher breakdown rate in operation

6. The PRIMARY function of the thermostat in the cooling system of an automobile engine is to 6.____

   A. control the operating temperature of the engine
   B. keep the operating temperature of the engine as low as possible
   C. provide the proper amount of heat for the heater
   D. retain engine heat when the engine gets hot

7. The PRIMARY purpose of the condenser in the ignition circuit of a gasoline engine is to 7.____

   A. boost the ignition voltage
   B. rectify the ignition voltage
   C. adjust the coil voltage
   D. reduce arcing at the distributor breaker points

8. The PRIMARY purpose of the differential in the rear drive train of an automotive vehicle is to allow each of the rear wheels to 8.____

A. rotate at different speeds
B. go in reverse
C. rotate with maximum torque
D. absorb road shocks

9. When an automobile engine does not start on a damp day, the trouble is MOST likely in the ______ system. 9.____

A. ignition
B. cooling
C. fuel
D. lubricating

10. The battery of an automobile is prevented from discharging back through the alternator by the blocking action of the 10.____

A. commutator
B. diodes
C. brushes
D. slip rings

11. The master cylinder in an automobile is actuated by the 11.____

A. steering column
B. brake pedal
C. clutch plate
D. cam shaft

Questions 12-17.

DIRECTIONS: Questions 12 through 17 are to be answered SOLELY on the basis of the following passage.

The basic hand-operated hoisting device is the tackle or purchase, consisting of a line called a fall, reeved through one or more blocks.

To hoist a load of given size, you must set up a rig with a safe working load equal to or in excess of the load to be hoisted. In order to do this, you must be able to calculate the safe working load of a single part of line of given size; the safe working load of a given purchase which contains a line of given size; and the minimum size of hooks or shackles which you must use in a given type of purchase to hoist a given load. You must also be able to calculate the thrust which a given load will exert on a gin pole or a set of shears inclined at a given angle; the safe working load which a spar of a given size, used as a gin pole or as one of a set of shears, will sustain; and the stress which a given load will set up in the back guy of a gin pole, or in the back guy of a set of shears, inclined at a given angle.

12. The above passage refers to the lifting of loads by means of 12.____

A. erected scaffolds
B. manual rigging devices
C. power-driven equipment
D. conveyor belts

13. It can be concluded from the above passage that a set of shears serves to 13.____

A. absorb the force and stress of the working load
B. operate the tackle
C. contain the working load
D. compute the safe working load

14. According to the above passage, a spar can be used for a 14.____

A. back guy B. block C. fall D. gin pole

15. According to the above passage, the rule that a user of hand-operated tackle MUST follow is to make sure that the safe working load is AT LEAST 15.____

A. equal to the weight of the given load
B. twice the combined weight of the block and falls
C. one-half the weight of the given load
D. twice the weight of the given load

16. According to the above passage, the two parts that make up a tackle are 16.____

A. back guys and gin poles
B. blocks and falls
C. rigs and shears
D. spars and shackle

17. According to the above passage, in order to determine whether it is safe to hoist a particular load, you MUST 17.____

A. use the maximum size hooks
B. time the speed to bring a given load to a desired place
C. calculate the forces exerted on various types of rigs
D. repeatedly lift and lower various loads

18. If you do not understand the operation of some special tool which is used in your work, your BEST procedure would be to 18.____

A. study up on its operation at home
B. ask a maintainer to explain its operation
C. ask another helper to explain its operation
D. bother nobody and expect to pick up a little more knowledge each time you use the tool

19. For winter servicing of a gasoline engine, it is BEST to use an oil that 19.____

A. has a low SAE number
B. has a high SAE number
C. has a very heavy consistency
D. contains few additive detergents

20. If a wheel has turned through an angle of 180°, then it has made ______ revolution(s). 20.____

A. 1/4 B. 1/2 C. 1/8 D. 18

21. The crankshaft in a gasoline engine is PRIMARILY used to 21.____

A. change reciprocating motion to rotary motion
B. operate the valve lifters
C. supply power to each cylinder
D. function as a flywheel

22. Assume that a mechanic is using a powder-actuated tool and the cartridge misfires. According to recommended safe practices regarding a misfired cartridge, the FIRST course of action the mechanic should take is to 22.____

   A. place the misfired cartridge carefully into a metal container filled with water
   B. carefully reload the tool with the misfired cartridge and try it again
   C. immediately bury the misfired cartridge at least two feet in the ground
   D. remove the wadding from the misfired cartridge and empty the powder into a pail of sand

23. The purpose of the ignition coil in a gasoline engine is PRIMARILY to 23.____

   A. smooth the voltage
   B. raise the voltage
   C. raise the current
   D. smooth the current

24. Vapor lock in a vehicle with a gasoline engine is caused by excessive heat. To prevent vapor lock, it may be necessary to relocate 24.____

   A. the ignition system
   B. the cooling system
   C. the starter motor
   D. a part of the fuel line

25. To accurately measure the small gap between relay contacts, it is BEST to use a(n) 25.____

   A. depth gauge
   B. *GO-NO GO* gauge
   C. feeler gauge
   D. inside caliper

KEY (CORRECT ANSWERS)

1.	C	11.	B
2.	A	12.	B
3.	C	13.	A
4.	D	14.	D
5.	B	15.	A
6.	A	16.	B
7.	D	17.	C
8.	A	18.	B
9.	A	19.	A
10.	B	20.	B

21. A
22. A
23. B
24. D
25. C

TEST 2

DIRECTIONS: Each question or incomplete statement is followed by several suggested answers or completions. Select the one that BEST answers the question or completes the statement. *PRINT THE LETTER OF THE CORRECT ANSWER IN THE SPACE AT THE RIGHT.*

1. Of the following, the MOST important reason for having a vehicle preventive maintenance and history card is 1.____

   A. for use in making vehicle assignments
   B. to check whether the drivers are completing their assignments
   C. for use as a control device in scheduling maintenance
   D. as a means for projecting future maintenance expenses

2. In his efforts to maintain standards of performance, a shop manager uses a system of close supervision to detect or catch errors. 2.____
   In OPPOSITE method of accomplishing the same objective is to employ a program which

   A. instills in each employee a pride of workmanship to do the job correctly the first time
   B. groups each job according to the importance to the overall objectives of the program
   C. makes the control of quality the responsibility of an inspector
   D. emphasizes that there is a *one* best way for an employee to do a specific job

3. Assume that after taking over a repair shop, a shop manager feels that he is taking too much time maintaining records. 3.____
   He should

   A. temporarily assign this job to one of his senior repair crew chiefs
   B. get together with his supervisor to determine if all these records are needed
   C. stop keeping those records which he believes are unnecessary
   D. spend a few additional hours each day until his records are current

4. In order to apply performance standards to employees engaged in repair shop activities, a shop manager must FIRST 4.____

   A. allow workers to decide for themselves the way to do the job
   B. determine what is acceptable as satisfactory work
   C. separate the more difficult tasks from the simpler tasks
   D. stick to an established work schedule

5. The term *preventative maintenance* is used to identify a plan whereby 5.____

   A. equipment is serviced according to a regular schedule
   B. equipment is serviced as soon as it fails
   C. equipment is replaced as soon as it becomes obsolete
   D. all equipment is replaced periodically

6. The ratio of air to gasoline in an automobile engine is controlled by the 6.____

A. gas filter
B. fuel pump
C. fuel injector
D. intake manifold

7. *Energizer* is another name given to the 7.____

A. automobile battery
B. fluorescent fixture ballast
C. battery charger
D. generator shunt field

8. Wearshoes may be found on 8.____

A. circuit breakers
B. automobile brake systems
C. snow plows
D. door sills

9. An oscilloscope is an instrument used in 9.____

A. measuring noise levels
B. displaying waveforms of electrical signals
C. indicating the concentrations of pollutants in air
D. photographing high-speed events

10. Assume that a brake pedal of a truck goes to the floorboard when depressed. The one of the following that could cause this condition Is 10.____

A. a leak in the hydraulic lines
B. a clogged hydraulic line
C. scored drums
D. glazed linings

11. The universal joints of an automobile are located on the 11.____

A. suspension springs
B. steering linkages
C. wheel cylinders
D. drive shaft

12. The MAIN purpose of a flexible coupling is to connect two shafts which are 12.____

A. of different diameters
B. of different shapes
C. not in exact alignment
D. of different material

13. When using a standard measuring micrometer, starting with a zero reading, one complete counterclockwise revolution of the sleeve will give a reading of _______ inch. 13.____

A. .001
B. .010
C. .025
D. .250

14. If a nut is to be tightened to an exact specified value of inch-lbs., the wrench to use is a _______ wrench. 14.____

A. spanner
B. box
C. lock-jaw
D. torque

15. Common permanent type anti-freezes for automobile cooling systems are MAINLY 15.____

A. alcohol
B. methanol
C. ethylene glycol
D. trichloroethylene

16. The function of the fuel injector on a gasoline engine is to 16.____

A. mix the air and gasoline properly
B. filter the fuel
C. filter the air to engine
D. pump the gasoline into the cylinder

17. If a car owner complains that the battery in his car is constantly running dry, the item that should be checked FIRST is the 17.____

A. fan belt
B. generator
C. voltage regulator
D. relay

18. On MOST modern automobiles, foot brake pressure is transmitted to the brake drums by 18.____

A. air pressure
B. mechanical linkage
C. hydraulic fluid
D. electromagnetic force

19. Assume that the engine of a car remains cold even though it is run for a period of time. The part that is MOST likely at fault is the 19.____

A. heat bypass valve
B. thermostat
C. heater control
D. choke

20. A rectifier changes 20.____

A. DC to AC
B. AC to DC
C. single-phase power to three-phase power
D. battery power to three-phase power

21. Continuity in a de-energized electrical circuit may be checked with a(n) 21.____

A. voltmeter
B. ohmmeter
C. neon tester
D. rheostat

22. Of the following crankcase oils, the one that should be used in sub-zero weather is SAE 22.____

A. 10W
B. 20W
C. 20
D. 30

23. Caster in an automobile is an adjustment in the 23.____

A. ignition system
B. drive-shaft
C. rear differential
D. front suspension

24. If the spark plugs in an engine run too hot, the result is MOST likely that 24.____

A. oil and carbon compounds will accumulate on the insulators
B. the electrodes will wear rapidly
C. the timing will be retarded
D. the ignition coil may become damaged

25. A low reading on the oil pressure gauge of a gasoline engine may mean that the 25.____

A. engine bearings are too tight
B. crankcase oil level is too low
C. transmission oil level is too low
D. transmission oil needs changing

KEY (CORRECT ANSWERS)

1. C	11. D
2. A	12. C
3. B	13. C
4. B	14. D
5. A	15. C
6. C	16. A
7. A	17. C
8. C	18. C
9. B	19. B
10. A	20. B

21. B
22. A
23. D
24. B
25. B

TEST 3

DIRECTIONS: Each question or incomplete statement is followed by several suggested answers or completions. Select the one that BEST answers the question or completes the statement. *PRINT THE LETTER OF THE CORRECT ANSWER IN THE SPACE AT THE RIGHT.*

1. To remove a slotted collar having internal threads from a shaft, the BEST of the following wrenches to use is a(n) ______ wrench. 1.____

   A. Allen B. Stillson C. socket D. spanner

2. When using a heavy jack placed on the ground to raise a heavy load, it is important to place a sturdy, flat board under the jack PRIMARILY in order to 2.____

   A. facilitate placing the jack under the load
   B. reduce the jacking effort
   C. prevent the jack from slipping out from under the load
   D. decrease the jacking height

3. The pulley wheels of a block and tackle are commonly called 3.____

   A. stocks B. swivels C. sheaves D. guides

4. If the diameter of a machined part must be 1.035 ± 0.003", then it is ACCEPTABLE if it measures 4.____

   A. 1.031" B. 1.032" C. 1.039" D. 1.335"

5. The type of threads for ordinary screws are USUALLY the ______ type. 5.____

   A. square B. buttress C. *V* D. Acme

6. Of the following actions a repair shop manager can take to determine if the vehicles used in his shop are being utilized properly, the one which will give him the LEAST meaningful information is 6.____

   A. conducting an analysis of vehicle assignments
   B. reviewing the number of miles travelled by each vehicle with and without loads
   C. recording the unloaded weights of each vehicle
   D. comparing the amount of time vehicles are parked at job sites with the time required to travel to and from job sites

7. For a shop manager, the MOST important reason that equipment which is used infrequently should be considered for disposal is that 7.____

   A. the time required for its maintenance could be better used elsewhere
   B. such equipment may cause higher management to think that your shop is not busy
   C. the men may resent having to work on such equipment
   D. such equipment usually has a higher breakdown rate in operation

8. In an automotive gasoline engine, the camshaft is used PRIMARILY to 8.____

A. drive the transmission
B. operate the valve lifters
C. change the reciprocating motion of the pistons to rotary motion
D. operate the choke mechanism

9. A magnetic motor starter is to be controlled with momentary start-stop pushbuttons at two locations. 9.____
The number of control wires required, respectively, in the conduit between the controller and the first station and in the conduit between the two stations is ______ and ______.

A. 3; 3 B. 4; 4 C. 3; 4 D. 2; 4

10. If the scale on a shop drawing is 1/2 inch to the foot, then the length of a part which measures 4 1/2 inches long on the drawing has a length of APPROXIMATELY ______ feet. 10.____

A. 2 1/8 B. 4 1/4 C. 8 1/2 D. 10 3/4

11. It is important to use safety shoes PRIMARILY to guard the feet against 11.____

A. tripping hazards
B. heavy falling objects
C. shock hazards
D. mud and dirt

12. When using a wrench to tighten a bolt, it is considered bad practice to extend the handle of the wrench with a pipe for added leverage PRIMARILY because 12.____

A. the pipe may break
B. the bolt head may be broken off
C. more space will be needed to turn the wrench with the pipe on it
D. no increase in leverage is obtained in this manner

13. The liquid solution in an electrical storage battery MOST commonly is 13.____

A. alkali
B. acid
C. pure distilled water
D. copper sulphate

14. Manifolds on an internal combustion engine are used 14.____

A. to mount the engine to the frame
B. for cooling the engine
C. in the carburetor
D. to conduct gases into and out of the engine

15. The energy stored by a storage battery is commonly given in 15.____

A. volts
B. amperes
C. ampere-hours
D. kilowatts

16. Vapor lock occurs in automobile 16.____

A. gas tanks
B. crankcases
C. transmissions
D. carburetors

17. The instrument generally used to determine the specific gravity of a lead-acid storage battery is the 17.____

A. ammeter
B. voltmeter
C. ohmmeter
D. hydrometer

18. A tachometer is an instrument that is used to measure 18.____

A. horizontal distances
B. radial distances
C. current in electric circuits
D. motor speed

19. A material that is commonly used as a lining for bearings in order to reduce friction is 19.____

A. magnesium
B. cast iron
C. babbitt
D. carborundum

20. In a motor having sleeve bearings, bearing wear can be checked by measuring the air-gap clearance between the armature and the 20.____

A. pole pieces
B. commutator
C. bearing
D. brushes

21. A revolution counter applied to the end of a rotating shaft reads 100 when a stopwatch is started and 850 after 90 seconds. 21.____
The shaft is rotating at a speed of ______ rpm.

A. 500
B. 633
C. 750
D. 950

22. If a kink develops in a wire rope, it would be BEST to 22.____

A. hammer out the kink with a lead hammer
B. straighten out the kink by putting it in a vise and applying sufficient pressure
C. discard the portion of rope containing the kink
D. keep the rope in use and allow the kink to work itself out

23. The one of the following flat drive-belts that gives the BEST service in dry places is a(n) _______ belt. 23.____

A. rawhide
B. oak-tanned
C. chrome-tanned
D. semirawhide

24. The letter representing the standard V-belt section which has the lowest horsepower-per-belt rating is 24.____

A. E
B. C
C. B
D. A

25. The criteria governing preventive maintenance of vehicles require that all of the following be done at certain intervals. 25.____
The one which must be done MOST frequently is

A. changing the engine oil
B. changing the engine oil filter
C. checking the radiator coolant level
D. rotating the tires

26. The one of the following that should NOT be lubricated is a(n) 26.____

A. spur gear train
B. motor commutator
C. roller chain drive
D. automobile axle

27. The one of the following oils that has the LOWEST viscosity is S.A.E. 27.____

A. 70
B. 50
C. 20
D. 10W

28. The one of the following V-belt sections which has the HIGHEST horsepower-per-belt rating is ______ section. 28.____

A. A
B. B
C. C
D. D

29. The one of the following transmission devices which should be oiled MOST often is the 29.____

A. V-belt
B. roller chain
C. rigid coupling
D. clutch plate

30. The one of the following statements concerning lubricating oil which is CORRECT is: 30.____

A. SAE 10 is heavier and more viscous than SAE 30
B. Diluting lubricating oil with gasoline increases its viscosity
C. Oil reduces friction between moving parts
D. In hot weather, thin oil is preferable to heavy oil

KEY (CORRECT ANSWERS)

1.	D	16.	D
2.	C	17.	D
3.	C	18.	D
4.	B	19.	C
5.	C	20.	A
6.	C	21.	A
7.	A	22.	C
8.	B	23.	B
9.	C	24.	D
10.	C	25.	C
11.	B	26.	B
12.	B	27.	D
13.	B	28.	D
14.	D	29.	B
15.	C	30.	C

EXAMINATION SECTION

TEST 1

DIRECTIONS: Each question or incomplete statement is followed by several suggested answers or completions. Select the one that BEST answers the question or completes the statement. *PRINT THE LETTER OF THE CORRECT ANSWER IN THE SPACE AT THE RIGHT.*

1. If a carburetor drips continually, the MOST likely cause is a 1.____
   A. loose Venturi tube B. needle valve not seating
   C. loose idle set screw D. float set too low

2. The part used to control the ratio of air and gasoline in a truck engine is the 2.____
   A. bogie B. filter C. carburetor D. pump

3. During cranking, all electrical energy is supplied by the 3.____
   A. alternator B. battery C. generator D. engine

4. A device for storing electric charges is known as a(n) 4.____
   A. commutator B. condenser C. capacitance D. exciter

5. Hydraulic brake fluid is a mixture of _____ and _____. 5.____
   A. kerosene; engine oil B. mineral oil; denatured alcohol
   C. castor oil; denatured alcohol D. ethelene glycol; mineral oil

6. When you are servicing the air brake chambers located at each wheel, the bolts and nuts holding the diaphragm plates should be tightened 6.____
   A. more tightly on the pressure plate than on the non-pressure plate
   B. more tightly on the non-pressure plate than on the pressure plate
   C. with only sufficient pressure to insure an air-tight seal
   D. with as much pressure as possible

7. The temperature gauge indicates the temperature of the 7.____
   A. air surrounding the engine B. water surrounding the cylinders
   C. oil in the crankcase D. pistons

8. Air drawn into the cooling system through the pump or hoses causes 8.____
   A. better cooling of the water B. the water to stop circulating
   C. a boost in the circulation D. rusting of the cylinder block

9. Diesel fuel filter elements on an International Harvester or Allis-Chalmers tractor are USUALLY serviced when too dirt for continued use by 9.____
   A. washing in kerosene B. steam cleaning
   C. washing in carbon tetrachloride D. oiling

10. To find out if a cylinder of a diesel engine is firing, it is necessary to 10.____
A. remove the fuel pump
B. disconnect the vent valve
C. remove the vent valve
D. prime the injection pump

11. In diesel engines, piston rings are held against the side of the cylinder PRIMARILY by 11.____
A. gas pressure behind the ring
B. thermal expansion of the ring
C. an oil wedge behind the ring
D. spring forces within the ring itself

12. In addition to lighter weight, the PRINCIPAL advantage of aluminum alloy pistons in diesel engines is that 12.____
A. piston rings have less tendency to collect sludge and stick
B. they have a much higher heat transfer rate than cast iron pistons
C. they expand less under heat and thus reduce liner wear
D. area for area, they are stronger than cast iron

13. All the refrigerant now used for automotive air conditioners is R 13.____
A. 10
B. 12
C. 18
D. 22

14. When the right front wheel is turned 20º to the left, the left front wheel should turn APPROXIMATELY _____ degrees. 14.____
A. 16
B. 18
C. 20
D. 24

15. In placing a new tire and a well-worn tire on dual wheels, it is BEST to place 15.____
A. the new tire on the inside
B. the worn tire on the inside
C. either tire on the inside; it makes no difference
D. the tires separately

16. The color of iron at welding heat is USUALLY a 16.____
A. creamy white
B. dull yellow
C. light yellow
D. light red

17. The _____ raring method measures the amount of current a battery can supply steadily for 20 hours, with no cell falling below 1.75 volts. 17.____
A. cold-cranking
B. reserve-capacity
C. watts
D. ampere-hour

18. In an automotive gasoline engine, the camshaft is used PRIMARILY to 18.____
A. drive the transmission
B. operate the valve lifters
C. change the reciprocating motion of the pistons to rotary motion
D. operate the choke mechanism

19. The PRIMARY function of the thermostat in the cooling system of an automobile engine is to 19.____
A. control the operating temperature of the engine
B. keep the operating temperature of the engine as low as possible
C. provide the proper amount of heat for the heater
D. retain engine heat when the engine gets hot

20. The PRIMARY purpose of the condenser in the ignition circuit of a gasoline engine is to 20.____
    A. boost the ignition voltage
    B. rectify the ignition voltage
    C. adjust the coil voltage
    D reducing arcing of the distributor breaker points

21. The PRIMARY purpose of the differential in the rear drive train of an automotive vehicle is to allow each of the rear wheels to 21.____
    A. rotate at different speeds
    B. go in reverse
    C. rotate with maximum torque
    D. absorb road shocks

22. Of the following, the BEST tool to use for securely tightening a one-inch standard hexagonal nut is a(n) 22.____
    A. monkey wrench
    B. open-end wrench
    C. Stillson wrench
    D. pair of heavy duty pliers

23. The purpose of the ignition coil in a gasoline engine is PRIMARILY to 23.____
    A. smooth the voltage
    B. raise the voltage
    C. raise the current
    D. smooth the current

24. Vapor lock in a vehicle with a gasoline engine is caused by excessive heat. To prevent vapor lock, it may be necessary to relocate 24.____
    A. the ignition system
    B. the cooling system
    C. the starter motor
    D. a part of the fuel line

25. It is important to use safety shoes PRIMARILY to guard the feet against 25.____
    A. tripping hazards
    B. heavy falling objects
    C. shock hazards
    D. mud and dirt

KEY (CORRECT ANSWERS)

1. B
2. C
3. B
4. B
5. C
6. C
7. B
8. D
9. A
10. B
11. D
12. C
13. B
14. D
15. D
16. A
17. B
18. B
19. A
20. D
21. A
22. B
23. B
24. D
25. B

TEST 2

DIRECTIONS: Each question or incomplete statement is followed by several suggested answers or completions. Select the one that BEST answers the question or completes the statement. *PRINT THE LETTER OF THE CORRECT ANSWER IN THE SPACE AT THE RIGHT.*

1. Which of the following is a PROBABLE result of a malfunctioning PCV valve? 1.____
   A. High fuel tank pressure
   B. Improper idling
   C. Noisy engine valves
   D. High fuel consumption

2. When a car goes into overdrive, the _____ gear is held stationary. 2.____
   A. pinion
   B. ring
   C. sun
   D. planetary

3. A puller is NOT commonly used to remove or install 3.____
   A. valves
   B. gears
   C. pulleys
   D. bearings

4. An engine turbocharger draws its energy from 4.____
   A. ignition spark
   B. engine fan airflow
   C. cylinder combustion
   D. hot exhaust gases

5. A four-gas automotive emissions analyzer will NOT measure the presence of 5.____
   A. HC
   B. CO
   C. CO_2
   D. NO

6. An automotive cylinder head is attached to the 6.____
   A. bearing saddle
   B. pan rail
   C. boss
   D. block deck

7. Which of the following is a DISADVANTAGE associated with a magnetic reluctance crankshaft position sensor that is used in a microprocessor-based control/diagnostic system? 7.____
   A. Inability to directly measure crankshaft position
   B. Inability to exploit flywheel rotation
   C. Requires additional installation of a harmonic damper
   D. Inability to set engine timing statically

8. Which valve train component CANNOT be used on overhead cam engines? 8.____
   A. Finger follower
   B. Bucket follower
   C. Tappet
   D. Rocker arm

9. Which of the following would likely be indicated by uneven firing voltages that are displayed on an oscilloscope? 9.____
   A. Worn plug electrodes
   B. Condenser failure
   C. Arcing contact points
   D. Point contact failure

10. Power steering systems typically use each of the following types of pumps EXCEPT 10.____
    A. vane
    B. diaphragm
    C. roller
    D. slipper

11. Most exhaust gas analyzers used in emission control maintenance indicate the percentage of _____ in the exhaust. 11._____
   A. HC B. CO C. NO D. CO_2

12. What is the term for the portion of a cam that has a constant diameter, and does not produce lift as it rotates? 12._____
   A. Offset B. Nose circle C. Flank circle D. Radial circle

13. In a microprocessor-based control/diagnostic system, which type of sensor uses the compound zirconia oxide? 13._____
   A. MAP B. Throttle angle
   C. EGO D. Knock

14. Which measuring device is MAINLY used to find open circuits and excessive resistance by imposing a bypass on a portion of the existing circuit? 14._____
   A. Digital multimeter B. Jumper wires
   C. Test light D. Continuity tester

15. If a car engine is operating at 1500 rpm, at what speed (rpm) is the distributor running? 15._____
   A. 750 B. 1500 C. 3000 D. 4500

16. Throttle body fuel injection refers to 16._____
   A. the insertion of fuel below the throttle plate
   B. unregulated fuel flow
   C. a continuous flow fuel injection
   D. a form of fuel metering actuator used in microprocessor-based control/diagnostic systems

17. Which of the following conditions in the valve train is NOT consistent with the *open valve* position in engine operation? 17._____
   A. Upward oil flow
   B. Plunger extended
   C. Slight leakage between plunger and body
   D. Ball check valve closed

18. What is the term for projections on a plate or disc that interlock in hub or drum slots? 18._____
   A. Drive lugs B. Toe cams
   C. Axial teeth D. Plate threads

19. Which of the following conditions is a POSSIBLE result of evaporation control system failure? 19._____
   A. Collapsed fuel tank B. High fuel tank pressure
   C. Improper idle D. Vapor low from air cleaner

20. Each of the following is a problem commonly associated with improper casting angles EXCEPT 20.____
   A. pulling to one side
   B. hard steering
   C. high speed instability
   D. rapid tire wear

21. In a microprocessor-based control/diagnostic system, which type of crankshaft position sensor is located in the distributor? 21.____
   A. Optical
   B. Ignition timing
   C. Hall-effect
   D. Magnetic reluctance

22. When using a short finder to trace a short circuit, which of the following steps should be performed FIRST? 22.____
   A. Turn on all switches in a series with the circuit being tested
   B. Move the short finder meter along circuit wiring
   C. Remove the blown fuse while leaving the battery connected
   D. Connect the pulse unit of short finder across the fuse terminals

23. In a fuel injection system, which type of pump is used PRIMARILY as a transfer pump? 23.____
   A. Rotary
   B. Diaphragm
   C. Turbine
   D. Roller

24. What type of electrical connectors are used to permanently join two stripped wire ends? 24.____
   A. Crimp
   B. Flat blade
   C. Butt
   D. Snap-splice

25. Discharges from the _____ appear as high voltage surges on an oscilloscope tester. 25.____
   A. distributor
   B. contact points
   C. coil high-tension terminal
   D. battery

KEY (CORRECT ANSWERS)

1. B
2. C
3. A
4. D
5. D

6. D
7. D
8. C
9. A
10. B

11. B
12. C
13. C
14. B
15. A

16. D
17. B
18. A
19. D
20. D

21. C
22. C
23. B
24. C
25. C

EXAMINATION SECTION

TEST 1

DIRECTIONS: Each question or incomplete statement is followed by several suggested answers or completions. Select the one that BEST answers the question or completes the statement. *PRINT THE LETTER OF THE CORRECT ANSWER IN THE SPACE AT THE RIGHT.*

1. All of the following are probable causes of an engine's failure to start EXCEPT 1.____
   A. cylinders not wired in proper order
   B. poor coolant circulation
   C. resistance unit burned out
   D. defective condenser

2. In an *expert* system for offboard computer diagnosis, which stage of knowledge acquisition in developing problem-solving rules occurs FIRST? 2.____
   A. Implementation B. Identification
   C. Formalization D. Conceptualization

3. Some suspension units consist of tandem axles joined by a single cross support that also acts as a vertical pivot for the entire unit. 3.____
   These units are known as
   A. axials B. field frames C. bogies D. helicals

4. In automotive electronics, the fractional duration that ignition points are closed is known as 4.____
   A. slip B. gain C. dwell D. delay

5. A brake system's warning lights may be tested by 5.____
   A. testing the bulbs with an ohmmeter
   B. depressing the brake pedal and opening a wheel cylinder bleeder screw
   C. jumping the wires at the brake distributor switch assembly
   D. testing the system with an ammeter

6. Of the following procedures performed prior to grinding a valve seat, which should be performed FIRST? 6.____
   A. Reaming B. Adjusting C. Cleaning D. Replacement

7. What type of clutch is responsible for controlling a car's air conditioning compressor? 7.____
   A. Centrifugal B. Free-wheeling
   C. Magnetic D. Mechanical

8. Which of the following is a DISADVANTAGE associated with onboard computer diagnostic systems? 8.____
   A. Inability to incorporate self-diagnosis
   B. Limited number of systems available for diagnosis
   C. Cannot be manually activated
   D. Inability to detect intermittent failures

9. Which parts in a motor or generator contact the rotating armature commutator or rings? 9.____
   A. Cams B. Brushes C. Rod caps D. Bushings

10. What is the MAIN advantage associated with the use of offboard computer diagnostic systems? 10.____
   A. Decreased task load
   B. Continuous testing intervals
   C. Can be manually activated by the driver
   D. Capable of simultaneous multiple diagnoses

11. An EGO sensor used in a microprocessor-based control/diagnostic system 11.____
   A. is perfectly linear
   B. is unaffected by temperature
   C. has two different output levels, depending on the fuel mixture
   D. is unaffected by engine exhaust levels

12. To what drive train component is the ring gear in the differential bolted? 12.____
   A. Drive pinion B. Axle shaft
   C. Differential case D. Carrier

13. What is transmitted by the slip rings on an automotive alternator? 13.____
   A. Alternating current to the field coils
   B. Alternating current from the stator windings
   C. Direct current from the field coils
   D. Direct current to the alternator output terminals

14. Which of the following is a PROBABLE cause of an engine's missing at low speed? 14.____
   A. Poor compression B. Leaky head gasket
   C. Carbon deposits in cylinders D. Loose flywheel

15. In order for an onboard computer diagnostic system to detect a failure in the cars electronic system, the failure must be 15.____
   A. associated with engine performance
   B. intermittent
   C. symptomatic
   D. nonreversible

16. What is the term for the part of a shaft which rotates in a bearing? 16.____
   A. Lunette B. Journal C. Jackshaft D. Kingpin

17. What is the USUAL steering gear reduction for passenger vehicles? 17.____
_____-to-1.
A. 2 B. 4 C. 8 D. 12

18. What is indicated by a low reading from 5 to 10 on an engine vacuum test? 18.____
A. Broken piston ring B. Weak cylinders
C. Late valve timing D. Valve sticking

19. Which of the following is NOT a component of the automotive power train? 19.____
A. Steering gear B. Clutch
C. Transmission D. Differential

20. Which instrument is NORMALLY used to check the condition of a resistance spark plug? 20.____
A. Voltmeter B. Ohmmeter C. Ammeter D. Potentiometer

21. Which device is used to measure the resistance of a circuit or electrical machine? 21.____
A. Ohmmeter B. Voltmeter C. Resistor D. Ammeter

22. What reading will appear on an infrared meter which indicates a failure of the catalytic converter? _____ HC/ ____ CO 22.____
A. Low; high B. Low; low C. High; low D. High; high

23. In automatic transmissions, the servo 23.____
A. operates the shifter valves
B. applies the clutch
C. applies the bands
D controls the output from the variable vane pump

24. If an onboard diagnostic system's fault code indicates that the O_2 sensor is not ready, all of the following are possible causes EXCEPT 24.____
A. O_2 sensor is not functioning correctly
B. defective connections or leads
C. lack of O_2 contacting sensor
D. control unit is not processing O_2 signal

25. The mechanical compressor in a car's air conditioning system is driven by 25.____
A. an electric motor B. the axles
C. the propeller shaft D. the crankshaft

KEY (CORRECT ANSWERS)

1.	B	11.	C
2.	B	12.	C
3.	C	13.	C
4.	C	14.	A
5.	B	15.	D
6.	C	16.	B
7.	C	17.	B
8.	D	18.	C
9.	B	19.	A
10.	A	20.	B

21.	A
22.	C
23.	C
24.	C
25.	D

TEST 2

DIRECTIONS: Each question or incomplete statement is followed by several suggested answers or completions. Select the one that BEST answers the question or completes the statement. *PRINT THE LETTER OF THE CORRECT ANSWER IN THE SPACE AT THE RIGHT.*

1. When installing disc brake linings, a hammer should be used to 1.____
   A. tighten the shoe retainer
   B. seat the pads in the calipers
   C. shape the pads
   D. remove the linings

2. What engine component is lubricated by the oil squirt hole in the connecting rod? 2.____
   A. Connecting rod bearing
   B. Crankshaft
   C. Cylinder wall
   D. Piston pin

3. Which of the following is a PROBABLE cause of backfiring through a carburetor? 3.____
   A. Short circuit in switch
   B. Water in gasoline
   C. Overheating
   D. Sticky thermostat

4. What is the GREATEST danger associated with hydraulic braking systems? 4.____
   A. Uneven braking
   B. Defective metering valve
   C. Loss of brake fluid
   D. Dirty or clogged wheel cylinder

5. Under what conditions must an engine be operated during a cylinder balance test? 5.____
   A. With the spark plugs firing, one at a time, at 1500 rpm
   B. With all plugs shorted but two which fire at non-simultaneous equal intervals
   C. At idle speed, with all plugs shorted but two which fire at non-simultaneous equal intervals
   D. At idle speed, with the spark plugs shorted, one at a time

6. Which of the following is a requisite property of brake fluid? 6.____
   A. Has detergents for keeping hoses unobstructed
   B. High wetting characteristics
   C. High viscosity
   D. High boiling point and low freezing point

7. What is measured by the mass airflow sensor in a microprocessor-based control/diagnostic system? The 7.____
   A. rate at which air is flowing into an engine
   B. composition of a given mass of air
   C. rate at which exhaust is flowing out of an engine
   D. density of atmospheric air

8. What is placed at the joint of a steel frame in order to strengthen the joint? 8.____
   A. Wobble plate
   B. Gusset plate
   C. Jackshaft
   D. Lint pin

9. What is indicated if a combustion meter reading is 10% higher with the air cleaner in place than when the air cleaner has been removed? 9.____
   A. Clogged injectors
   B. Dirty air cleaner
   C. Clogged vent
   D. Normal operation

10. Which of the following is a PROBABLE cause of an engine failing to stop? 10.____
   A. Lack of pressure on gasoline tank
   B. Disconnected magneto ground
   C. High altitude
   D. Spark plug gaps too wide

11. Automotive sensors used in computer-operated diagnostic or control systems typically see changes in each of the following EXCEPT 11.____
   A. electrical signals
   B. temperature
   C. position
   D. pressure

12. What type of feeler gauge should be used to set the gap on a new set of spark plugs? 12.____
   A. Flat
   B. Ramp-type
   C. Wire
   D. Round

13. Intake and exhaust manifolds are built with their walls contacting each other in order to 13.____
   A. reduce atomization
   B. pre-heat the fuel mixture
   C. facilitate valve action
   D. conserve space

14. Fuel tank vapors stored in the charcoal canister 14.____
   A. are released to the atmosphere through a bleed valve
   B. are released to the atmosphere through a port in the canister
   C. are cycled back into the fuel tank
   D. become part of the fuel mixture when the engine is started

15. The information handled by a computerized engine control system flows from 15.____
   A. computer to sensor to display
   B. actuator to display to computer
   C. sensor to computer to actuator
   D. sensor to display to computer

16. In a car with manual transmission, spring pressure clamps the friction disc between the pressure plate and the _____ when the clutch is engaged. 16.____
   A. sun gear
   B. reaction plate
   C. flywheel
   D. differential

17. If the insulation material used with a crimp connector on electric wiring is coded red, what range of gauges is considered typical? 17.____
   A. 10-12
   B. 12-18
   C. 14-16
   D. 18-22

18. An air conditioning system's expansion valve controls the 18.____
   A. pressure of refrigerant in the compressor
   B. temperature of refrigerant in the condenser
   C. amount of refrigerant in the evaporator
   D. temperature of air in the car's interior

19. Each of the following is a probable cause of engine overheating EXCEPT 19.____
   A. slipping fan belt
   B. frozen radiator
   C. improper valve timing
   D. short circuit in distributor rotor

20. When using a short finder to trace a short circuit, which of the following steps should be performed LAST? 20.____
   A. Turn on all switches in a series with the circuit being tested
   B. Move the short finder meter along circuit wiring
   C. Remove the blown fuse while leaving the battery connected
   D. Connect the pulse unit of short finder across the fuse terminals

21. If a light load test is performed on a battery and the battery shows less than 1.95 volts in all cells, then the battery 21.____
   A. is overly discharged
   B. should be replaced
   C. needs charging
   D. is in good condition

22. A *thermistor* is a 22.____
   A. newly-developed type of transistor
   B. device for regulating engine temperature
   C. temperature control system operated by a car passenger
   D. semiconductor temperature sensor

23. An *expert* system for offboard computer diagnosis differs from other computerized diagnostic systems because it is capable of 23.____
   A. carrying out several diagnostic operations at once
   B. recommending repair procedures
   C. determining the causes of problems without manual assistance
   D. sensing faults in a circuitry that is not related to engine performance

24. In which type of engine are all valve contained in the cylinder block? 24.____
   A. V-type
   B. Two-stroke
   C. F-head
   D. L-head

25. The function of a MAP sensor in a microprocessor-based control/diagnostic system is to 25.____
   A. sense anomalous changes in a vehicle's traveling direction
   B. measure changes in mean atmospheric pressure
   C. measure manifold absolute pressure
   D. measure fluctuations in manifold air flow

KEY (CORRECT ANSWERS)

1.	C	11.	A
2.	C	12.	C
3.	D	13.	B
4.	C	14.	D
5.	B	15.	C
6.	D	16.	C
7.	A	17.	D
8.	B	18.	C
9.	B	19.	C
10.	B	20.	B

21.	A
22.	D
23.	B
24.	D
25.	C

TEST 3

DIRECTIONS: Each question or incomplete statement is followed by several suggested answers or completions. Select the one that BEST answers the question or completes the statement. *PRINT THE LETTER OF THE CORRECT ANSWER IN THE SPACE AT THE RIGHT.*

1. What is indicated by a sudden periodic drop of 1 or 2 points during a vacuum test on a car's engine? 1.____
   A. Spark plug failure B. Damaged distributor cap
   C. Coil failure D. Low oil pressure

2. A stud axle is articulated to an axle-beam or steering head by means of a 2.____
   A. journal B. kingpin C. gusset plate D. poppet

3. Which of the following should be checked FIRST when examining a front suspension? 3.____
   A. Kingpins B. Steering connections
   C. Bumper and frame level D. Suspension arm pivots

4. Which of the following procedures involving a combustion efficiency tester will detect manifold leaks? 4.____
   A. Accelerating the engine to fast speed and checking for meter deflection
   B. Pumping the accelerator and checking for instant response in the combustion meter
   C. Applying a kerosene/oil mixture to the flange and manifold gaskets and checking for meter deflection
   D. Placing the engine on full choke and checking for meter deflection

5. If a car's battery is always fully charged, which of the following should be checked? 5.____
   A. Short circuiting in alternator B. Output amperage of the alternator
   C. volt regulator output D. Volt regulator points

6. Which of the following are companion cylinders in a car's V-8 engine? 6.____
   A. 1 and 8 B. 2 and 8 C. 3 and 4 D. 2 and 7

7. Which of the following is a PROBABLE cause of firing in a car's muffler? 7.____
   A. Too rich a fuel mixture
   B. Carbon deposits in cylinder
   C. Improperly adjusted valve tappets
   D. Water in gasoline

8. What is the MAJOR benefit associated with the use of *expert* offboard computer diagnostic systems? 8.____
   A. High task load capability
   B. Continuous testing intervals
   C. Consistent application of problem-solving strategies
   D. Simultaneous multiple-system capability

9. Which type of valve is used to sense how fast a vehicle is traveling? 9.____
A. Throttle B. Governor C. Manual D. Modulator

10. A two-unit alternator is composed of a 10.____
A. voltage limiter and current limiter
B. current limiter and reverse current relay
C. voltage limiter and field relay
D. current limiter and field relay

11. Which type of gears are used for the forward speeds of fully synchronized standard transmissions? 11.____
A. Helical B. Double helical
C. Hypoid D. Spur

12. When checking a circuit for voltage drop, which of the following steps should be performed FIRST? 12.____
A. Select the voltmeter range just above the battery circuit
B. Connect the positive lead of the voltmeter to the end of the wire closest to the battery
C. Connect the negative lead of the voltmeter to the end of the wire farthest from the battery
D. Switch on the circuit

13. Each of the following is a probable cause of engine knocking EXCEPT 13.____
A. compression too low B. loose piston
C. spark too far advanced D. engine overheated

14. In what portion of an *expert* system for offboard computer diagnosis are logical operation performed? 14.____
A. Domain B. Inference engine
C. Knowledge base D. Interface

15. In the propeller shaft of an automotive transmission, a universal joint allows variation in the 15.____
A. speed of rotation B. angle of drive
C. length of the shaft D. direction of rotation

16. Which of the following is a POSSIBLE use for an engine analyzer? 16.____
A. Setting the choke B. Measuring intake fuel flow rate
C. Setting ignition points D. Measuring fuel mixture

17. What is the term for the smaller of two mating or meshing gears? 17.____
A. Linch B. Master C. Pinion D. Pilot

18. Conditioned air in an automotive air conditioning system is cooled as it passes through the 18.____
A. condenser B. evaporator C. compressor D. receiver

19. In order to determine the correct valve timing of an engine, the opening and closing of the valves should be measured in reference to the 19.____
    A. cylinder compression ratio
    B. fuel mixing jets
    C. distributor setting
    D. piston position

20. In modern engines using computer-based control systems, diagnosis is performed 20.____
    A. with an engine analyzer
    B. with a timing light only
    C. with a timing light and voltmeter
    D. in the digital control system

21. What is the MOST probable cause of a car drifting from side to side on a level road? 21.____
    A. Bent steering arm
    B. Tight shock absorber
    C. Loose steering connections
    D. Bent axle

22. Which device, as part of a special type of pump, drives plunger back and forth as it rotates, producing the pumping action? 22.____
    A. Trunnion
    B. Torus
    C. Camber link
    D. Wobble plate

23. In a microprocessor-based control/diagnostic system, a typical engine crankshaft angular position sensor is MOST effectively located on the 23.____
    A. camshaft
    B. crankshaft
    C. compressor pulley
    D. flywheel

24. Which type of gauge will allow a mechanic to MOST accurately set the proper electrode gap on a spark plug? 24.____
    A. Flat feeler
    B. Round wire feeler
    C. Square wire feeler
    D. Dial

25. What type of logical rule bases are programmed into MOST expert diagnostic systems? 25.____
    A. Either/or
    B. Set/subset
    C. If/then
    D. Inductive

KEY (CORRECT ANSWERS)

1. A
2. B
3. C
4. C
5. C

6. B
7. A
8. C
9. B
10. C

11. A
12. B
13. A
14. B
15. B

16. C
17. C
18. B
19. D
20. D

21. C
22. D
23. B
24. B
25. C

WORK SCHEDULING

EXAMINATION SECTION
TEST 1

DIRECTIONS: Each question or incomplete statement is followed by several suggested answers or completions. Select the one that BEST answers the question or completes the statement. *PRINT THE LETTER OF THE CORRECT ANSWER IN THE SPACE AT THE RIGHT.*

Questions 1-6.

DIRECTIONS: Questions 1 through 6 are to be answered SOLELY on the basis of the information given in the ELEVATOR OPERATORS' WORK SCHEDULE shown below.

ELEVATOR OPERATORS' WORK SCHEDULE

Operator	Hours of Work	A.M. Relief Period	Lunch Hour	P.M. Relief Period
Anderson	8:30-4:30	10:20-10:30	12:00-1:00	2:20-2:30
Carter	8:00-4:00	10:10-10:20	11:45-12:45	2:30-2:40
Daniels	9:00-5:00	10:20-10:30	12:30-1:30	3:15-3:25
Grand	9:30-5:30	11:30-11:40	1:00-2:00	4:05-4:15
Jones	7:45-3:45	9:45-9:55	11:30-12:30	2:05-2:15
Lewis	9:45-5:45	11:40-11:50	1:15-2:15	4:20-4:30
Nance	8:45-4:45	10:50-11:00	12:30-1:30	3:05-3:15
Perkins	8:00-4:00	10:00-10:10	12:00-1:00	2:40-2:50
Russo	7:45-3:45	9:30-9:40	11:30-12:30	2:10-2:20
Smith	9:45-5:45	11:45-11:55	1:15-2:15	4:05-4:15

1. The two operators who are on P.M. relief at the SAME time are 1.____

   A. Anderson and Daniels B. Carter and Perkins
   C. Jones and Russo D. Grand and Smith

2. Of the following, the two operators who have the SAME lunch hour are 2.____

   A. Anderson and Perkins B. Daniels and Russo
   C. Grand and Smith D. Nance and Russo

3. At 12:15, the number of operators on their lunch hour is 3.____

   A. 3 B. 4 C. 5 D. 6

4. The operator who has an A.M. relief period right after Perkins and a P.M. relief period right before Perkins is 4.____

   A. Russo B. Nance C. Daniels D. Carter

5. The number of operators who are scheduled to be working at 4:40 is 5.____

   A. 5 B. 6 C. 7 D. 8

6. According to the schedule, it is MOST correct to say that 6.____
   A. no operator has a relief period during the time that another operator has a lunch hour
   B. each operator has to wait an identical amount of time between the end of lunch and the beginning of P.M. relief period
   C. no operator has a relief period before 9:45 or after 4:00
   D. each operator is allowed a total of 1 hour and 20 minutes for lunch hour and relief periods

---

KEY (CORRECT ANSWERS)

1. D
2. A
3. C
4. D
5. A
6. D

TEST 2

DIRECTIONS: Each question or incomplete statement is followed by several suggested answers or completions. Select the one that BEST answers the question or completes the statement. *PRINT THE LETTER OF THE CORRECT ANSWER IN THE SPACE AT THE RIGHT.*

Questions 1-7.

DIRECTIONS: Questions 1 through 7 are to be answered SOLELY on the basis of the time sheet and instructions given below.

The following time sheet indicates the times that seven laundry workers arrived and left each day for the week of August 23. The times they arrived for work are shown under the heading IN, and the times they left are shown under the heading OUT. The letter (P) indicates time which was used for personal business. Time used for this purpose is charged to annual leave. Lunch time is one-half hour from noon to 12:30 P.M. and is not accounted for on this time record.

The employees on this shift are scheduled to work from 8:00 A.M. to 4:00 P.M. Lateness is charged to annual leave. Reporting after 8:00 A.M. is considered late.

	MON.		TUES.		WED.		THURS.		FRI.	
	AM IN	PM OUT	AM IN	PM OUT	AM IN	PM OUT	AM IN	PM OUT	AM IN	PM OUT
Baxter	7:50	4:01	7:49	4:07	8:00	4:07	8:20	4:00	7:42	4:03
Gardner	8:02	4:00	8:20	4:00	8:05	3:30(P)	8:00	4:03	8:00	4:07
Clements	8:00	4:04	8:03	4:01	7:59	4:00	7:54	4:06	7:59	4:00
Tompkins	7:56	4:00	Annual leave		8:00	4:07	7:59	4:00	8:00	4:01
Wagner	8:04	4:03	7:40	4:00	7:53	4:04	8:00	4:09	7:53	4:00
Patterson	8:00	2:30(P)	8:15	4:04	Sick leave		7:45	4:00	7:59	4:04
Cunningham	7:43	4:02	7:50	4:00	7:59	4:02	8:00	4:10	8:00	4:00

1. Which one of the following laundry workers did NOT have any time charged to annual leave or sick leave during the week? 1.____

   A. Gardner B. Clements C. Tompkins D. Cunningham

2. On which day did ALL the laundry workers arrive on time? 2.____

   A. Monday B. Wednesday C. Thursday D. Friday

3. Which of the following laundry workers used time to take care of personal business? 3.____

   A. Baxter and Clements
   B. Patterson and Cunningham
   C. Gardner and Patterson
   D. Wagner and Tompkins

4. How many laundry workers were late on Monday? 4.____

   A. 1 B. 2 C. 3 D. 4

5. Which one of the following laundry workers arrived late on three of the five days? 5.____

   A. Baxter B. Gardner C. Wagner D. Patterson

6. The percentage of laundry workers reporting to work late on Tuesday is MOST NEARLY 6.____

   A. 15% B. 25% C. 45% D. 50%

7. The percentage of laundry workers that were absent for an entire day during the week is MOST NEARLY 7.____

   A. 6% B. 9% C. 15% D. 30%

KEY (CORRECT ANSWERS)

1. D
2. D
3. C
4. B
5. B
6. C
7. D

TEST 3

Questions 1-9.

DIRECTIONS: Questions 1 through 9 are to be answered SOLELY on the basis of the following information and timesheet given below.

The following is a foreman's timesheet for his crew for one week. The hours worked each day or the reason the man was off on that day are shown on the sheet. *R* means rest day. *A* means annual leave. *5* means sick leave. Where a man worked only part of a day, both the number of hours worked and the number of hours taken off are entered. The reason for absence is entered in parentheses next to the number of hours taken off.

Name	Saturday	Sunday	Monday	Tuesday	Wednesday	Thursday	Friday
Smith	R	R	7	7	7	3 4(A)	7
Jones	R	7	7	7	7	7	R
Green	R	R	7	7	S	S	S
White	R	R	7	7	A	7	7
Doe	7	7	7	7	7	R	R
Brown	R	R	A	7	7	7	7
Black	R	R	S	7	7	7	7
Reed	R	R	7	7	7	7	S
Roe	R	R	A	7	7	7	7
Lane	7	R	R	7	7	A	S

1. The caretaker who worked EXACTLY 21 hours during the week is 1.____

   A. Lane B. Roe C. Smith D. White

2. The TOTAL number of hours worked by all caretakers during the week is 2.____

   A. 268 B. 276 C. 280 D. 288

3. The two days of the week on which MOST caretakers were off are 3.____

   A. Thursday and Friday
   B. Friday and Saturday
   C. Saturday and Sunday
   D. Sunday and Monday

4. The day on which three caretakers were off on sick leave is 4.____

   A. Monday B. Friday C. Saturday D. Sunday

5. The two workers who took LEAST time off during the week are 5.____

   A. Doe and Reed
   B. Jones and Doe
   C. Reed and Smith
   D. Smith and Jones

6. The caretaker who worked the LEAST number of hours during the week is 6.____

   A. Brown B. Green C. Lane D. Roe

7. The caretakers who did NOT work on Thursday are 7.____

   A. Doe, White, and Smith
   B. Green, Doe, and Lane
   C. Green, Doe, and Smith
   D. Green, Lane, and Smith

8. The day on which one caretaker worked ONLY 3 hours is 8.____

   A. Friday B. Saturday C. Thursday D. Wednesday

9. The day on which ALL caretakers worked is 9.____

   A. Monday B. Thursday C. Tuesday D. Wednesday

KEY (CORRECT ANSWERS)

1. A
2. B
3. C
4. B
5. B

6. B
7. B
8. C
9. C

TEST 4

Questions 1-6.

DIRECTIONS: Questions 1 through 6 are to be answered SOLELY on the basis of the table below which shows the initial requests made by staff for vacation. It is to be used with the RULES AND GUIDELINES to make the decisions and judgments called for in each of the questions.

VACATION REQUESTS FOR THE ONE YEAR PERIOD FROM MAY 1, YEAR X THROUGH APRIL 30, YEAR Y				
Name	Work Assignment	Date Appointed	Accumulated Annual Leave Days	Vacation Periods Requested
DeMarco	MVO	Mar. 2003	25	May 3-21; Oct. 25-Nov. 5
Moore	Dispatcher	Dec. 1997	32	May 24-June 4; July 12-16
Kingston	MVO	Apr. 2007	28	May 24-June 11; Feb. 7-25
Green	MVO	June 2006	26	June 7-18; Sept. 6-24
Robinson	MVO	July 2008	30	June 28-July 9; Nov. 15-26
Reilly	MVO	Oct. 2009	23	July 5-9; Jan. 31-Mar. 3
Stevens	MVO	Sept. 1996	31	July 5-23; Oct. 4-29
Costello	MVO	Sept. 1998	31	July 5-30; Oct. 4-22
Maloney	Dispatcher	Aug. 1992	35	July 5-Aug. 6; Nov. 1-5
Hughes	Director	Feb. 1990	38	July 26-Sept. 3
Lord	MVO	Jan. 2010	20	Aug. 9-27; Feb. 7-25
Diaz	MVO	Dec. 2009	28	Aug. 9-Sept. 10
Krimsky	MVO	May 2006	22	Oct. 18-22: Nov. 22-Dec. 10

<u>RULES AND GUIDELINES</u>

1. The two Dispatchers cannot be on vacation at the same time, nor can a Dispatcher be on vacation at the same time as the Director.

2. For the period June 1 through September 30, not more than three MVO's can be on vacation at the same time.

3. For the period October 1 through May 31, not more than two MVO's at a time can be on vacation.

4. In cases where the same vacation time is requested by too many employees for all of them to be given the time under the rules, the requests of those who have worked the longest will be granted.

5. No employee may take more leave days than the number of annual leave days accumulated and shown in the table.

6. All vacation periods shown in the table and described in the questions below begin on a Monday and end on a Friday.

7. Employees work a five-day week (Monday through Friday). They are off weekends and holidays with no charges to leave balances. When a holiday falls on a Saturday or Sunday, employees are given the following Mondav off without charge to annual leave.

8. Holidays:

May 31	October 25	January 1
July 4	November 2	February 12
September 6	November 25	February 21
October 11	December 25	February 21

9. An employee shall be given any part of his initial requests that is permissible under the above rules and shall have first right to it despite any further adjustment of schedule.

---

1. Until adjustments in the vacation schedule can be made, the vacation dates that can be approved for Krimsky are 1.____
   A. Oct. 18-22; Nov. 22-Dec. 10
   B. Oct. 18-22; Nov. 29-Dec. 10
   C. Oct. 18-22 *only*
   D. Nov. 22-Dec. 10 *only*

2. Until adjustments in the vacation schedule can be made, the vacation dates that can be approved for Maloney are 2.____
   A. July 5-Aug. 6; Nov. 1-5
   B. July 5-23; Nov. 1-5
   C. July 5-9; Nov. 1-5
   D. Nov. 1-5 *only*

3. According to the table, Lord wants a vacation in August and another in February. Until adjustments in the vacation schedule can be made, he can be allowed to take ______ of the August vacation and ______ of the February vacation. 3.____
   A. all; none
   B. all; almost half
   C. almost all; almost half
   D. almost half; all

4. Costello cannot be given all the vacation he has requested because 4.____
   A. the MVO's who have more seniority than he has have requested time he wishes
   B. he does not have enough accumulated annual leave
   C. a dispatcher is applying for vacation at the same time as Costello
   D. there are five people who want vacation in July

5. According to the table, how many leave days will DeMarco be charged for his vacation from October 25 through November 5? 5.____
   A. 10
   B. 9
   C. 8
   D. 7

6. How many leave days will Moore use if he uses the requested vacation allowable to him under the rules? 6.____
   A. 9
   B. 10
   C. 14
   D. 15

KEY (CORRECT ANSWERS)

1. D
2. B
3. A
4. B
5. C
6. A

TEST 5

Questions 1-8.

DIRECTIONS: Questions 1 through 8 are to be answered SOLELY on the basis of Charts I, II, III, and IV. Assume that you are the supervisor of Operators R, S, T, U, V, W, and X, and it is your responsibility to schedule their lunch hours.

The charts each represent a possible scheduling of lunch hours during a lunch period from 11:30 - 2:00. An operator-hour is one hour of time spent by one operator. Each box on the chart represents one half-hour. The boxes marked L represent the time when each operator is scheduled to have her lunch hour. For example, in Chart I, next to Operator R, the boxes for 11:30 - 12:00 and 12:00 -12:30 are marked L. This means that Operator R is scheduled to have her lunch hour from 11:30 to 12:30.

I

	11:30-12:00	12:00-12:30	12:30-1:00	1:00-1:30	1:30-2:00
R	L	L			
S		L	L		
T		L	L		
U			L	L	
V			L	T	
W				L	L
X				L	L

II

	11:30-12:00	12:00-12:30	12:30-1:00	1:00-1:30	1:30-2:00
R				L	L
S		L	L		
T	L	L			
U		L	L		
V				L	L
W				L	L
X		L	L		

III

	11:30-12:00	12:00-12:30	12:30-1:00	1:00-1:30	1:30-2:00
R	L	L			
S				L	L
T	L	L			
U			L	L	
V	L	L			
W			L	L	
X			L	L	

IV

	11:30-12:00	12:00-12:30	12:30-1:00	1:00-1:30	1:30-2:00
R	L	L			
S	L	L			
T		L	L		
U			L	L	
V				L	L
W				L	L
X			L	L	

1. If, under the schedule represented in Chart II, Operator R has her lunch hour changed to 12:30-1:30, that leaves how many operator-hours of phone coverage from 1:00-2:00? 1.___

   A. 2 B. 2 1/2 C. 3 D. 4 1/2

2. If Operator S asks you whether she and Operator T may have the same lunch hour, you could accommodate her by using the schedule in Chart 2.___

   A. I B. II C. III D. IV

3. From past experience you know that the part of the lunch period when the phones are busiest is from 12:30-1:30. Which chart shows the BEST phone coverage from 12:30 to 1:30? 3.___

   A. I B. II C. III D. IV

4. At least three operators have the same lunch hour according to Chart(s) 4.___

   A. II and III
   B. II and IV
   C. III only
   D. IV only

5. Which chart would provide the POOREST phone coverage during the period 12:00-1:30, based on total number of operator-hours from 12:00 to 1:30? 5.____

   A. I B. II C. III D. IV

6. Which chart would make it possible for U, W, and X to have the same lunch hour? 6.____

   A. I B. II C. III D. IV

7. The portion of the lunch period during which the telephones are least busy is 11:30-12:30.
   Which chart is MOST likely to have been designed with that fact in mind? 7.____

   A. I B. II C. III D. IV

8. Assume that you have decided to use Chart IV to schedule your operators' lunch hours on a specific day. Operator T asks you if she can have her lunch hour changed to 1:00-2:00.
   If you grant her request, how many operators will be working during the period 12:00 to 12:30? 8.____

   A. 1 B. 2 C. 4 D. 5

KEY (CORRECT ANSWERS)

1. D
2. A
3. B
4. A
5. A
6. C
7. C
8. D

TEST 6

Questions 1-13.

DIRECTIONS: Questions 1 through 13 consist of a statement. You are to indicate whether the statement is TRUE (T) or FALSE (F). *PRINT THE LETTER OF THE CORRECT ANSWER IN THE SPACE AT THE RIGHT.* Questions 1 through 13 are to be answered SOLELY on the basis of the information given in the table below.

DEPARTMENT OF FERRIES ATTENDANTS WORK ASSIGNMENT - JULY 2003					
Name	Year Employed	Ferry Assigned	Hours of Work	Lunch Period	Davs Off
Adams	1999	Hudson	7 AM - 3 PM	11-12	Fri. and Sat.
Baker	1992	Monroe	7 AM - 3 PM	11-12	Sun. and Mon.
Gunn	1995	Troy	8 AM - 4 PM	12-1	Fri. and Sat.
Hahn	1989	Erie	9 AM - 5 PM	1-2	Sat. and Sun.
King	1998	Albany	7 AM - 3 PM	11-12	Sun. and Mon.
Nash	1993	Hudson	11 AM - 7 PM	3-4	Sun. and Mon.
Olive	2003	Fulton	10 AM - 6 PM	2-3	Sat. and Sun.
Queen	2002	Albany	11 AM - 7 PM	3-4	Fri. and Sat.
Rose	1990	Troy	11 AM - 7 PM	3-4	Sun. and Mon.
Smith	1991	Monroe	10 AM - 6 PM	2-3	Fri. and Sat.

1. The chart shows that there are only five (5) ferries being used. 1.____
2. The attendant who has been working the LONGEST time is Rose. 2.____
3. The Troy has one more attendant assigned to it than the Erie. 3.____
4. Two (2) attendants are assigned to work from 10 P.M. to 6 A.M. 4.____
5. According to the chart, no more than one attendant was hired in any year. 5.____
6. The NEWEST employee is Olive. 6.____
7. There are as many attendants on the 7 to 3 shift as on the 11 to 7 shift. 7.____
8. MOST of the attendants have their lunch either between 12 and 1 or 2 and 3. 8.____
9. All the employees work four (4) hours before they go to lunch. 9.____
10. On the Hudson, Adams goes to lunch when Nash reports to work. 10.____
11. All the attendants who work on the 7 to 3 shift are off on Saturday and Sunday. 11.____
12. All the attendants have either a Saturday or Sunday as one of their days off. 12.____
13. At least two (2) attendants are assigned to each ferry. 13.____

KEY (CORRECT ANSWERS)

1. F	6. T	11. F
2. F	7. T	12. T
3. T	8. F	13. F
4. F	9. T	
5. T	10. T	

EXAMINATION SECTION

TEST 1

DIRECTIONS: Each question or incomplete statement is followed by several suggested answers or completions. Select the one that BEST answers the question or completes the statement. *PRINT THE LETTER OF THE CORRECT ANSWER IN THE SPACE AT THE RIGHT.*

1. Of the following, the one MOST important quality required of a good supervisor is 1.____
   A. ambition B. leadership C. friendliness D. popularity

2. It is often said that a supervisor can delegate authority but never responsibility. This means MOST NEARLY that 2.____
   A. a supervisor must do his own work if he expects it to be done properly
   B. a supervisor can assign someone else to do his work, but in the last analysis, the supervisor himself must take the blame for any actions followed
   C. authority and responsibility are two separate things that cannot be borne by the same person
   D. it is better for a supervisor never to delegate his authority

3. One of your men who is a habitual complainer asks you to grant him a minor privilege. 3.____
   Before granting or denying such a request, you should consider
   A. the merits of the case
   B. that it is good for group morale to grant a request of this nature
   C. the man's seniority
   D. that to deny such a request will lower your standing with the men

4. A supervisory practice on the part of a foreman which is MOST likely to lead to confusion and inefficiency is for him to 4.____
   A. give orders verbally directly to the man assigned to the job
   B. issue orders only in writing
   C. follow up his orders after issuing them
   D. relay his orders to the men through co-workers

5. It would be POOR supervision on a foreman's part if he 5.____
   A. asked an experienced maintainer for his opinion on the method of doing a special job
   B. make it a policy to avoid criticizing a man in front of his co-workers
   C. consulted his assistant supervisor on unusual problems
   D. allowed a cooling-off period of several days before giving one of his men a deserved reprimand

6. Of the following behavior characteristics of a supervisor, the one that is MOST likely to lower the morale of the men he supervises is 6.____
   A. diligence
   B. favoritism
   C. punctuality
   D. thoroughness

7. Of the following, the BEST method of getting an employee who is not working up to his capacity to produce more work is to 7.____
   A. have another employee criticize his production
   B. privately criticize his production but encourage him to produce more
   C. criticize his production before his associates
   D. criticize his production and threaten to fire him

8. Of the following, the BEST thing for a supervisor to do when a subordinate has done a very good job is to 8.____
   A. tell him to take it easy
   B. praise his work
   C. reduce his workload
   D. say nothing because he may become conceited

9. Your orders to your crew are MOST likely to be followed if you 9.____
   A. explain the reasons for these orders
   B. warn that all violators will be punished
   C. promise easy assignments to those who follow these orders best
   D. say that they are for the good of the department

10. In order to be a good supervisor, you should 10.____
   A. impress upon your men that you demand perfection in their work at all times
   B. avoid being blamed for your crew's mistakes
   C. impress your superior with your ability
   D. see to it that your men get what they are entitled to

11. In giving instructions to a crew, you should 11.____
   A. speak in as loud a tone as possible
   B. speak in a coaxing, persuasive manner
   C. speak quietly, clearly, and courteously
   D. always use the word *please* when giving instructions

12. Of the following factors, the one which is LEAST important in evaluating an employee and his work is his 12.____
   A. dependability
   B. quantity of work done
   C. quality of work done
   D. education and training

13. When a District Superintendent first assumes his command, it is LEAST important for him at the beginning to observe 13.____
   A. how his equipment is designed and its adaptability
   B. how to reorganize the district for greater efficiency
   C. the capabilities of the men in the district
   D. the methods of operation being employed

14. When making an inspection of one of the buildings under your supervision, the BEST procedure to follow in making a record of the inspection is to 14.____
   A. return immediately to the office and write a report from memory
   B. write down all the important facts during or as soon as you complete the inspection
   C. fix in your mind all important facts so that you can repeat them from memory if necessary
   D. fix in your mind all important facts so that you can make out your report at the end of the day

15. Assume that your superior has directed you to make certain changes in your established procedure. After using this modified procedure on several occasions, you find that the original procedure was distinctly superior and you wish to return to it. 15.____
You should
   A. let your superior find this out for himself
   B. simply change back to the original procedure
   C. compile definite data and information to prove your case to your superior
   D. persuade one of the more experienced workers to take this matter up with your superior

16. An inspector visited a large building under construction. He inspected the soil lines at 9 A.M., water lines at 10 A.M., fixtures at 11 A.M., and did his office work in the afternoon. He followed the same pattern daily for weeks. 16.____
This procedure was
   A. *good*, because it was methodical and he did not miss anything
   B. *good*, because it gave equal time to all phases of the plumbing
   C. *bad*, because not enough time was devoted to fixtures
   D. *bad*, because the tradesmen knew when the inspection would occur

17. Assume that one of the foremen in a training course, which you are conducting, proposes a poor solution for a maintenance problem. 17.____
Of the following, the BEST course of action for you to take is to
   A. accept the solution tentatively and correct it during the next class meeting
   B. point out all the defects of this proposed solution and wait until somebody thinks of a better solution
   C. try to get the class to reject this proposed solution and develop a better solution
   D. let the matter pass since somebody will present a better solution as the class work proceeds

18. As a supervisor, you should be seeking ways to improve the efficiency of shop operations by means such as changing established work procedures. 18.____
The following are offered as possible actions that you should consider in changing established work procedures:
   I. Make changes only when your foremen agree to them
   II. Discuss changes with your supervisor before putting them into practice

III. Standardize any operation which is performed on a continuing basis
IV. Make changes quickly and quietly in order to avoid dissent
V. Secure expert guidance before instituting unfamiliar procedures
Of the following suggested answers, the one that describes the actions to be taken to change established work procedures is
A. I, IV, V B. II, III, V C. III, IV, V D. All of the above

19. A supervisor determined that a foreman, without informing his superior, delegated responsibility for checking time cards to a member of his gang. The supervisor then called the foreman into his office where he reprimanded the foreman. 19.____
This action of the supervisor in reprimanding the foreman was
A. *proper*, because the checking of time cards is the foreman's responsibility and should not be delegated
B. *proper*, because the foreman did not ask the supervisor for permission to delegate responsibility
C. *improper*, because the foreman may no longer take the initiative in solving future problems
D. *improper*, because the supervisor is interfering in a function which is not his responsibility

20. A capable supervisor should check all operations under his control. 20.____
Of the following, the LEAST important reason for doing this is to make sure that
A. operations are being performed as scheduled
B. he personally observes all operations at all times
C. all the operations are still needed
D. his manpower is being utilized efficiently

21. A supervisor makes it a practice to apply fair and firm discipline in all cases of rule infractions, including those of a minor nature 21.____
This practice should PRIMARILY be considered
A. *bad*, since applying discipline for minor violations is a waste of time
B. *good*, because not applying discipline for minor infractions can lead to a more serious erosion of discipline
C. *bad*, because employees do not like to be disciplined for minor violations of the rules
D. *good*, because violating any rule can cause a dangerous situation to occur

22. A maintainer would PROPERLY consider it poor supervisory practice for a foreman to consult with him on 22.____
A. which of several repair jobs should be scheduled first
B. how to cope with personal problems at home
C. whether the neatness of his headquarters can be improved
D. how to express a suggestion which the maintainer plans to submit formally

23. Assume that you have determined that the work of one of your foremen and the men he supervises is consistently behind schedule. When you discuss this situation with the foreman, he tells you that his men are poor workers and then complains that he must spend all of his time checking on their work. 23.____
The following actions are offered for your consideration as possible ways of solving the problem of poor performance of the foreman and his men:
I. Review the work standards with the foreman and determine whether they are realistic.
II. Tell the foreman that you will recommend him for the foreman's training course for retraining.
III. Ask the foreman for the names of the maintainers and then replace them as soon as possible.
IV. Tell the foreman that you expect him to meet a satisfactory level of performance.
V. Tell the foreman to insist that his men work overtime to catch up to the schedule.
VI. Tell the foreman to review the type and amount of training he has given the maintainers.
VII. Tell the foreman that he will be out of a job if he does not produce on schedule.
VIII. Avoid all criticism of the foreman and his methods.
Which of the following suggested answers CORRECTLY lists the proper actions to be taken to solve the problem of poor performance of the foreman and his men?
A. I, II, IV, VI B. I, III, V, VII C. II, III, VI, VIII D. IV, V, VI, VIII

24. When a conference or a group discussion is tending to turn into a *bull session* without constructive purpose, the BEST action to take is to 24.____
A. reprimand the leader of the bull session
B. redirect the discussion to the business at hand
C. dismiss the meeting and reschedule it for another day
D. allow the bull session to continue

25. Assume that you have been assigned responsibility for a program in which a high production rate is mandatory. From past experience, you know that your foremen do not perform equally well in the various types of jobs given to them. Which of the following methods should you use in selecting foremen for the specific types of work involved in the program? 25.____
A. Leave the method of selecting foremen to your supervisor
B. Assign each foreman to the work he does best
C. Allow each foreman to choose his own job
D. Assign each foreman to a job which will permit him to improve his own abilities

KEY (CORRECT ANSWERS)

1.	B	11.	C
2.	B	12.	D
3.	A	13.	B
4.	D	14.	B
5.	D	15.	C
6.	B	16.	D
7.	B	17.	C
8.	B	18.	B
9.	A	19.	A
10.	D	20.	B

21.	B
22.	A
23.	A
24.	B
25.	B

TEST 2

DIRECTIONS: Each question or incomplete statement is followed by several suggested answers or completions. Select the one that BEST answers the question or completes the statement. *PRINT THE LETTER OF THE CORRECT ANSWER IN THE SPACE AT THE RIGHT.*

1. A foreman who is familiar with modern management principles should know that the one of the following requirements of an administrator which is LEAST important is his ability to 1.____
   A. coordinate work
   B. plan, organize, and direct the work under his control
   C. cooperate with others
   D. perform the duties of the employees under his jurisdiction

2. When subordinates request his advice in solving problems encountered in their work, a certain chief occasionally answers the request by first asking the subordinate what he thinks should be done. 2.____
   This action by the chief is, on the whole,
   A. *desirable*, because it stimulates subordinates to give more thought to the solution of problems encountered
   B. *undesirable*, because it discourages subordinates from asking questions
   C. *desirable*, because it discourages subordinates from asking questions
   D. *undesirable*, because it undermines the confidence of subordinates in the ability of their supervisor

3. Of the following factors that may be considered by a unit head in dealing with the tardy subordinate, the one which should be given LEAST consideration is the 3.____
   A. frequency with which the employee is tardy
   B. effect of the employee's tardiness upon the work of other employees
   C. willingness of the employee to work overtime when necessary
   D. cause of the employee's tardiness

4. The MOST important requirement of a good inspectional report is that it should be 4.____
   A. properly addressed
   B. lengthy
   C. clear and brief
   D. spelled correctly

5. Building superintendents frequently inquire about departmental inspectional procedures. 5.____
   Of the following, it is BEST to
   A. advise them to write to the department for an official reply
   B. refuse as the inspectional procedure is a restricted matter
   C. briefly explain the procedure to them
   D. avoid the inquiry by changing the subject

6. Reprimanding a crew member before other workers is a 6.____
   A. *good* practice; the reprimand serves as a warning to the other workers
   B. *bad* practice; people usually resent criticism made in public
   C. *good* practice; the other workers will realize that the supervisor is fair
   D. *bad* practice; the other workers will take sides in the dispute

7. Of the following actions, the one which is LEAST likely to promote good work is for the group leader to 7.____
   A. praise workers for doing a good job
   B. call attention to the opportunities for promotion for better workers
   C. threaten to recommend discharge of workers who are below standard
   D. put into practice any good suggestion made by crew members

8. A supervisor notices that a member of his crew has skipped a routine step in his job. 8.____
   Of the following, the BEST action for the supervisor to take is to
   A. promptly question the worker about the incident
   B. immediately assign another man to complete the job
   C. bring up the incident the next time the worker asks for a favor
   D. say nothing about the incident but watch the worker carefully in the future

9. Assume you have been told to show a new worker how to operate a piece of equipment. 9.____
   Your FIRST step should be to
   A. ask the worker if he has any questions about the equipment
   B. permit the worker to operate the equipment himself while you carefully watch to prevent damage
   C. demonstrate the operation of the equipment for the worker
   D. have the worker read an instruction booklet on the maintenance of the equipment

10. Whenever a new man was assigned to his crew, the supervisor would introduce him to all other crew members, take him on a tour of the plant, tell him about bus schedules and places to eat. 10.____
    This practice is
    A. *good*; the new man is made to feel welcome
    B. *bad*; supervisors should not interfere in personal matters
    C. *good*; the new man knows that he can bring his personal problems to the supervisor
    D. *bad*; work time should not be spent on personal matters

11. The MOST important factor in successful leadership is the ability to 11.____
    A. obtain instant obedience to all orders
    B. establish friendly personal relations with crew members
    C. avoid disciplining crew members
    D. make crew members want to do what should be done

12. Explaining the reasons for departmental procedure to workers tends to 12.____
    A. waste time which should be used for productive purposes
    B. increase their interest in their work
    C. make them more critical of departmental procedures
    D. confuse them

13. If you want a job done well do it yourself. 13.____
    For a supervisor to follow this advice would be
    A. *good*; a supervisor is responsible for the work of his crew
    B. *bad*; a supervisor should train his men, not do their work
    C. *good*; a supervisor should be skilled in all jobs assigned to his crew
    D. *bad*; a supervisor loses respect when he works with his hands

14. When a supervisor discovers a mistake in one of the jobs for which his crew is responsible, it is MOST important for him to find out 14.____
    A. whether anybody else knows about the mistake
    B. who was to blame for the mistake
    C. how to prevent similar mistakes in the future
    D. whether similar mistakes occurred in the past

15. A supervisor who has to explain a new procedure to his crew should realize that questions from the crew USUALLY show that they 15.____
    A. are opposed to the new practice
    B. are completely confused by the explanation
    C. need more training in the new procedure
    D. are interested in the explanation

16. A good way for a supervisor to retain the confidence of his or her employees is to 16.____
    A. say as little as possible
    B. check work frequently
    C. make no promises unless they will be fulfilled
    D. never hesitate in giving an answer to any question

17. Good supervision is ESSENTIALLY a matter of 17.____
    A. patience in supervising workers
    B. care in selecting workers
    C. skill in human relations
    D. fairness in disciplining workers

18. It is MOST important for an employee who has been assigned a monotonous task to 18.____
    A. perform this task before doing other work
    B. ask another employee to help
    C. perform this task only after all other work has been completed
    D. take measures to prevent mistakes in performing the task

19. One of your employees has violated a minor agency regulation. 19.____
The FIRST thing you should do is
A. warn the employee that you will have to take disciplinary action if it should happen again
B. ask the employee to explain his or her actions
C. inform your supervisor and wait for advice
D. write a memo describing the incident and place it in the employee's personnel file

20. One of your employees tells you that he feels you give him much more work than the other employees, and he is having trouble meeting your deadlines. 20.____
You should
A. ask if he has been under a lot of non-work related stress lately
B. review his recent assignments to determine if he is correct
C. explain that this is a busy time, but you are dividing the work equally
D. tell him that he is the most competent employee and that is why he receives more work

21. A supervisor assigns one of his crew to complete a portion of a job. A short time later, the supervisor notices that the portion has not been completed. 21.____
Of the following, the BEST way for the supervisor to handle this is to
A. ask the crew member why he has not completed the assignment
B. reprimand the crew member for not obeying orders
C. assign another crew member to complete the assignment
D. complete the assignment himself

22. Supposes that a member of your crew complains that you are *playing favorites* in assigning work. 22.____
Of the following, the BEST method of handling the complaint is to
A. deny it and refuse to discuss the matter with the worker
B. take the opportunity to tell the worker what is wrong with his work
C. ask the worker for examples to prove his point and try to clear up any misunderstanding
D. promise to be more careful in making assignments in the future

23. A member of your crew comes to you with a complaint. After discussing the matter with him, it is clear that you have convinced him that his complaint was not justified. 23.____
At this point, you should
A. permit him to drop the matter
B. make him admit his error
C. pretend to see some justification in his complaint
D. warn him against making unjustified complaints

24. Suppose that a supervisor has in his crew an older man who works rather slowly. In other respects, this man is a good worker; he is seldom absent, works carefully, never loafs, and is cooperative. 24.____

The BEST way for the supervisor to handle this worker is to
A. try to get him to work faster and less carefully
B. give him the most disagreeable job
C. request that he be given special training
D. permit him to work at his own speed

25. Suppose that a member of your crew comes to you with a suggestion he thinks will save time in doing a job. You realize immediately that it won't work. Under these circumstances, your BEST action would be to 25.____
A. thank the worker for the suggestion and forget about it
B. explain to the worker why you think it won't work
C. tell the worker to put the suggestion in writing
D. ask the other members of your crew to criticize the suggestion

---

KEY (CORRECT ANSWERS)

1.	D	11.	D
2.	A	12.	B
3.	C	13.	B
4.	C	14.	C
5.	C	15.	D
6.	B	16.	C
7.	C	17.	C
8.	A	18.	D
9.	C	19.	B
10.	A	20.	B

21. A
22. C
23. A
24. D
25. B

SUPERVISION STUDY GUIDE

Social science has developed information about groups and leadership in general and supervisor-employee relationships in particular. Since organizational effectiveness is closely linked to the ability of supervisors to direct the activities of employees, these findings are important to executives everywhere.

IS A SUPERVISOR A LEADER?

First-line supervisors are found in all large business and government organizations. They are the men at the base of an organizational hierarchy. Decisions made by the head of the organization reach them through a network of intermediate positions. They are frequently referred to as part of the management team, but their duties seldom seem to support this description.

A supervisor of clerks, tax collectors, meat inspectors, or securities analysts is not charged with budget preparation. He cannot hire or fire the employees in his own unit on his say-so. He does not administer programs which require great planning, coordinating, or decision making.

Then what is he? He is the man who is directly in charge of a group of employees doing productive work for a business or government agency. If the work requires the use of machines, the men he supervises operate them. If the work requires the writing of reports, the men he supervises write them. He is expected to maintain a productive flow of work without creating problems which higher levels of management must solve. But is he a leader?

To carry out a specific part of an agency's mission, management creates a unit, staffs it with a group of employees and designates a supervisor to take charge of them. Management directs what this unit shall do, from time to time changes directions, and often indicates what the group should not do. Management presumably creates status for the supervisor by giving him more pay, a title, and special privileges.

Management asks a supervisor to get his workers to attain organizational goals, including the desired quantity and quality of production. Supposedly, he has authority to enable him to achieve this objective. Management at least assumes that by establishing the status of the supervisor's position, it has created sufficient authority to enable him to achieve these goals—not his goals, nor necessarily the group's, but management's goals.

In addition, supervision includes writing reports, keeping records of membership in a higher-level administrative group, industrial engineering, safety engineering, editorial duties, housekeeping duties, etc. The supervisor as a member of an organizational network, must be responsible to the changing demands of the management above him. At the same time, he must be responsive to the demands of the work group of which he is a member. He is placed in the difficult position of communicating and implementing new decisions, changed programs and revised production quotas for his work group, although he may have had little part in developing them.

It follows, then, that supervision has a special characteristic: achievement of goals, previously set by management, through the efforts of others. It is in this feature of the supervisor's job that we find the role of a leader in the sense of the following definition: *A leader is that person who most effectively influences group activities toward goal setting and goal achievements.*

This definition is broad. It covers both leaders in groups that come together voluntarily and in those brought together through a work assignment in a factory, store, or government agency. In the natural group, the authority necessary to attain goals is determined by the group membership and is granted by them. In the working group, it is apparent that the establishment of a supervisory position creates a predisposition on the part of employees to accept the authority of the occupant of that position. We cannot, however, assume that mere occupation confers authority sufficient to assure the accomplishment of an organization's goals.

Supervision is different, then, from leadership. The supervisor is expected to fulfill the role of leader but without obtaining a grant of authority from the group he supervises. The supervisor is expected to influence the group in the achieving of goals but is often handicapped by having little influence on the organizational process by which goals are set. The supervisor, because he works in an organizational setting, has the burdens of additional organizational duties and restrictions and requirements arising out of the fact that his position is subordinate to a hierarchy of higher-level supervisors. These differences between leadership and supervision are reflected in our definition: *Supervision is basically a leadership role, in a formal organization, which has as its objective the effective influencing of other employees.*

Even though these differences between supervision and leadership exist, a significant finding of experimenters in this field is that supervisors must be leaders to be successful.

The problem is: How can a supervisor exercise leadership in an organizational setting? We might say that the supervisor is expected to be a natural leader in a situation which does not come about naturally. His situation becomes really difficult in an organization which is more eager to make its supervisors into followers rather than leaders.

LEADERSHIP: NATURAL AND ORGANIZATIONAL

Leadership, in its usual sense of *natural* leadership, and supervision are not the same. In some cases, leadership embraces broader powers and functions than supervision; in other cases, supervision embraces more than leadership. This is true both because of the organization and technical aspects of the supervisor's job and because of the relatively freer setting and inherent authority of the natural leader.

The natural leader usually has much more authority and influence than the supervisor. Group members not only follow his command but prefer it that way. The employee, however, can appeal the supervisor's commands to his union or to the supervisor's superior or to the personnel office. These intercessors represent restrictions on the supervisor's power to lead.

The natural leader can gain greater membership involvement in the group's objectives, and he can change the objectives of the group. The supervisor can attempt to gain employee support only for management's objectives; he cannot set other objectives. In these instances leadership is broader than supervision.

The natural leader must depend upon whatever skills are available when seeking to attain objectives. The supervisor is trained in the administrative skills necessary to achieve management's goals. If he does not possess the requisite skills, however, he can call upon management's technicians.

A natural leader can maintain his leadership, in certain groups, merely by satisfying members' need for group affiliation. The supervisor must maintain his leadership by directing and organizing his group to achieve specific organizational goals set for him and his group by management. He must have a technical competence and a kind of coordinating ability which is not needed by many natural leaders.

A natural leader is responsible only to his group which grants him authority. The supervisor is responsible to management, which employs him, and also to the work group of which he is a member. The supervisor has the exceedingly difficult job of reconciling the demands of two groups frequently in conflict. He is often placed in the untenable position of trying to play two antagonistic roles. In the above instance, supervision is broader than leadership.

ORGANIZATIONAL INFLUENCES ON LEADERSHIP

The supervisor is both a product and a prisoner of the organization wherein we find him. The organization which creates the supervisor's position also obstructs, restricts, and channelizes the exercise of his duties. These influences extend beyond prescribed functional relationships to specific supervisory behavior. For example, even in a face-to-face situation involving one of his subordinates, the supervisor's actions are controlled to a great extent by his organization. His behavior must conform to the organization policy on human relations, rules which dictate personnel procedures, specific prohibitions governing conduct, the attitudes of his own superior, etc. He is not a free agent operating within the limits of his work group. His freedom of action is much more circumscribed than is generally admitted. The organizational influences which limit his leadership actions can be classified as structure, prescriptions, and proscriptions.

The organizational structure places each supervisor's position in context with other designated positions. It determines the relationships between his position and specific positions which impinge on his. The structure of the organization designates a certain position to which he looks for orders and information about his work. It gives a particular status to his position within a pattern of statuses from which he perceives that (1) certain positions are on a par, organizationally, with his, (2) other positions are subordinate, and (3) still others are superior.

The organizational structure determines those positions to which he should look for advice and assistance, and those positions to which he should give advice and assistance.

For instance, the organizational structure has predetermined that the supervisor of a clerical processing unit shall report to a supervisory position in a higher echelon. He shall have certain relationships with the supervisors of the work units which transmit work to and receive work from his unit. He shall discuss changes and clarification of procedures with certain staff units, such as organization and methods, cost accounting, and personnel. He shall consult supervisors of units which provide or receive special work assignments.

The organizational structure, however, establishes patterns other than those of the relationships of positions. These are the patterns of responsibility, authority, and expectations.

The supervisor is responsible for certain activities or results; he is presumably invested with the authority to achieve these. His set of authority and responsibility is interwoven with other sets to the end that all goals and functions of the organization are parceled out in small, manageable lots. This, of course, establishes a series of expectations: a single supervisor can perform his particular set of duties only upon the assumption that preceding or contiguous sets of duties have been, or are being carried out. At the same time, he is aware of the expectations of others that he will fulfill his functional role.

The structure of an organization establishes relationships between specified positions and specific expectations for these positions. The fact that these relationships and expectations are established is one thing; whether or not they are met is another.

PRESCRIPTIONS AND PROSCRIPTIONS

But let us return to the organizational influences which act to restrict the supervisor's exercise of leadership. These are the prescriptions and proscriptions generally in effect in all organizations, and those peculiar to a single organization. In brief these are the *thou shalt's* and the *thou shalt not's*.

Organizations not only prescribe certain duties for individual supervisory positions, they also prescribe specific methods and means of carrying out these duties and maintaining management-employee relations. These include rules, regulations, policy, and tradition. It does no good for the supervisor to say, *This seems to be the best way to handle such-and-such,* if the organization has established a routine for dealing with problems. For good or bad, there are rules that state that firings shall be executed in such a manner, accompanied by a certain notification; that training shall be conducted, and in this manner. Proscriptions are merely negative prescriptions; you may not discriminate against any employee because of politics or race; you shall not suspend any employee without following certain procedures and obtaining certain approvals.

Most of these prohibitions and rules apply to the area of interpersonal relations, precisely the area which is now arousing most interest on the part of administrators and managers. We have become concerned about the contrast between formally prescribed relationships and interpersonal relationships, and this brings us to the often discussed informal organization.

5

FORMAL AND INFORMAL ORGANIZATIONS

As we well know, the functions and activities of any organization are broken down into individual units of work called positions. Administrators must establish a pattern which will link these positions to each other and relate them to a system of authority and responsibility. Man-to-man are spelled out as plainly as possible for all to understand. Managers, then, build an official structure which we call the formal organization.

In these same organizations, employees react individually and in groups to institutionally determined roles. John, a worker, rides in the same carpool as Joe, a foreman. An unplanned communication develops. Harry, a machinist knows more about high-speed machining than his foreman or anyone else in his shop. An unofficial tool boss comes into being. Mary, who fought with Jane, is promoted over her. Jane now gives Mary's directions. A planned relationship fails to develop. The employees have built a structure which we call the informal organization.

> *Formal organization is a system of management-prescribed relations between positions in an organization.*
>
> *Informal organization is a network of unofficial relations between people in an organization.*

These definitions might lead us to the absurd conclusion that positions carry out formal activities and that employe4es spend their time in unofficial activities. We must recognize that organizational activities are in all cases carried out by people. The formal structure provides a needed framework within which interpersonal relations occur. What we call informal organization is the complex of normal, natural relations among employees. These personal relationships may be negative or positive. That is, they may impede or aid the achievement of organizational goals. For example, friendship between two supervisors greatly increases the probability of good cooperation and coordination between their sections. On the other hand, *buck passing* nullifies the formal structure by failure to meet a prescribed and expected responsibility.

It is improbable that an ideal organization exists where all activities are carried out in strict conformity to a formally prescribed pattern of functional roles. Informal organization arises because of the incompleteness and ambiguities in the network of formally prescribed relationships, or in response to the needs or inadequacies of supervisors or managers who hold prescribed functional roles in an organization. Many of these relationships are not prescribed by the organizational pattern; many cannot be prescribed; many should not be prescribed.

Management faces the problem of keeping the informal organization in harmony with the mission of the agency. One way to do this is to make sure that all employees have a clear understanding of and are sympathetic with that mission. The issuance of organizational charts, procedural manuals, and functional descriptions of the work to be done by divisions and sections helps communicate management's plans and goals. Issuances alone, of course, cannot do the whole job. They should be accompanied by oral discussion and explanation. Management must ensure that there is mutual understanding and acceptance of charts and procedures. More important is that management acquaint itself with the attitudes, activities, and peculiar brands of logic which govern the informal organization. Only through this type of knowledge can they and supervisors keep informal goals consistent with the agency mission.

SUPERVISION STATUS AND FUNCTIONAL ROLE

A well-established supervisor is respected by the employees who work with him. They defer to his wishes. It is clear that a superior-subordinate relationship has been established. That is, status of the supervisor has been established in relation to other employees of the same work group. This same supervisor gains the respect of employees when he behaves in as certain manner. He will be expected, generally, to follow the customs of the group in such matters as dress, recreation, and manner of speaking. The group has a set of expectations as to his behavior. His position is a functional role which carries with it a collection of rights and obligations.

The position of supervisor usually has a status distinct from the individual who occupies it: it is much like a position description which exists whether or not there is an incumbent. The status of a supervisory position is valued higher than that of an employee position both because of the functional role of leadership which is assigned to it and because of the status symbols of titles, rights, and privileges which go with it.

Social ranking, or status, is not simple because it involves both the position and the man. An individual may be ranked higher than others because of his education, social background, perceived leadership ability, or conformity to group customs and ideals. If such a man is ranked higher by the members of a work group than their supervisor, the supervisor's effectiveness may be seriously undermined.

If the organization does not build and reinforce a supervisor's status, his position can be undermined in a different way. This will happen when managers go around rather than through the supervisor or designate him as a straw boss, acting boss, or otherwise not a real boss.

Let us clarify this last point. A role, and corresponding status, establishes a set of expectations. Employees expect their supervisor to do certain things and to act in certain ways. They are prepared to respond to that expected behavior. When the supervisor's behavior does not conform to their expectations, they are surprised, confused, and ill-at-ease. It becomes necessary for them to resolve their confusion, if they can. They might do this by turning to one of their own members for leadership. If the confusion continues, or their attempted solutions are not satisfactory, they will probably become a poorly motivated, non-cohesive group which cannot function very well.

COMMUNICATION AND THE SUPERVISOR

In a recent survey, railroad workers reported that they rarely look to their supervisor for information about the company. This is startling, at least to us, because we ordinarily think of the supervisor as the link between management and worker. We expect the supervisor to be the prime source of information about the company. Actually, the railroad workers listed the supervisor next to last in the o5rder of their sources of information. Most surprising of all, the supervisors, themselves, stated that rumor and unofficial contacts were their principal sources of information. Here we see one of the reasons why supervisors may not be as effective as management desires.

The supervisor is not only being bypassed by his work group, he is being ignored, and his position weakened, by the very organization which is holding him responsible for the activities of his workers. If he is management's representative to the employee, then management has an obligation to keep him informed of its activities. This is necessary if he is to carry out his functions efficiently and maintain his leadership in the work group. The supervisor is expected to be a source of information; when he is not, his status is not clear, and employees are dissatisfied because he has not lived up to expectations.

By providing information to the supervisor to pass along to employees, we can strengthen his position as leader of the group, and increase satisfaction and cohesion within the group. Because he has more information than the other members, receives information sooner, and passes it along at the proper times, members turn to him as a source and also provide him with information in the hope of receiving some in return. From this, we can see an increase in group cohesiveness because:

- Employees are bound closer to their supervisor because he is *in the know.*
- There is less need to go outside the group for answers
- Employees will more quickly turn to the supervisor for enlightenment

The fact that he has the answers will also enhance the supervisor's standing in the eyes of his men. This increased status will serve to bolster his authority and control of the group and will probably result in improved morale and productivity.

The foregoing, of course, does not mean that all management information should be given out. There are obviously certain policy determinations and discussions which need not or cannot be transmitted to all supervisors. However, the supervisor must be kept as fully informed as possible so that he can answer questions when asked and can allay needless fears and anxieties. Further, the supervisor has the responsibility of encouraging employee questions and submissions of information. He must be able to present information to employees so that it is clearly understood and accepted. His attitude and manner should make it clear that he believes in what he is saying, that the information is necessary or desirable to the group, and that he is prepared to act on the basis of the information.

SUPERVISION AND JOB PERFORMANCE

The productivity of work groups is a product; employees' efforts are multiplied by the supervision they receive. Many investigators have analyzed this relationship and have discovered elements of supervision which differentiate high and low production groups. These researchers have identified certain types of supervisory practices which they classify as *employee-centered* and other types which they classify as *production centered.*

The difference between these two kinds of supervision lies not in specific practices but in the approach or orientation to supervision. The employee-centered supervisor directs most of his efforts toward increasing employee motivation. He is concerned more with realizing the potential energy of persons than with administrative and technological methods of increasing efficiency and productivity. He is the man who finds ways of causing employees to want to work harder with the same tools. These supervisors emphasize the personal relations between their employees and themselves.

Now, obviously, these pictures are overdrawn. No one supervisor has all the virtues of the ideal type of employee-centered supervisor. And, fortunately, no one supervisor has all the bad traits found in many production-centered supervisors. We should remember that the various practices that researchers have fond which distinguish these two kinds of supervision represent the many practices and methods of supervisors of all gradations between these extremes. We should be careful, too, of the implications of the labels attached to the two types. For instance, being production-centered is not necessarily bad, since the principal responsibility of any supervisor is maintaining the production level that is expected of his work group. Being employee-centered may not necessarily be good, if the only result is a happy, chuckling crew of loafers. To return to the researchers' findings, employee-centered supervisors:

- Recommend promotions, transfers, pay increases
- Inform men about what is happening in the company
- Keep men posted on how well they are doing
- Hear complaints and grievances sympathetically
- Speak up for subordinates

Production-centered supervisors, on the other hand, don't do those things. They check on employees more frequently, give more detailed and frequent instructions, don't give reasons for changes, and are more punitive when mistakes are made. Employee-centered supervisors were reported to contribute to high morale and high production, whereas production-centered supervision was associated with lower morale and less production.

More recent findings, however, show that the relationship between supervision and productivity is not this simple. Investigators now report that high production is more frequently associated with supervisory practices which combine employee-centered behavior with concern for production. (This concern is not the same, however, as anxiety about production, which is the hallmark of our production-centered supervisor.) Let us examine these apparently contradictory findings and the premises from which they are derived.

SUPERVISION AND MORALE

Why do supervisory activities cause high or low production? As the name implies, the activities of the employee-centered supervisor tend to relate him more closely and satisfactorily to his workers. The production-centered supervisor's practices tend to separate him from his group and to foster antagonism. An analysis of this difference may answer our question.

Earlier, we pointed out that the supervisor is a type of leader and that leadership is intimately related to the group in which it occurs We discover, now, that an employee-centered supervisor's primary activities are concerned with both his leadership and his group membership. Such a supervisor is a member of a group and occupies a leadership role in that group.

These facts are sometimes obscured when we speak of the supervisor as management's representative, or as the organizational link between management and the employee, or as the end of the chain of command. If we really want to understand what it is we expect of the supervisor, we must remember that he is the designated leader of a group of employees to whom he is bound by interaction and interdependence.

Most of his actions are aimed, consciously or unconsciously, at strengthening membership ties in the group. This includes both making members more conscious that he is a member of their group) and causing members to identify themselves more closely with the group. These ends are accomplished by:

- making the group more attractive to the worker: they find satisfaction of their needs for recognition, friendship, enjoyable work, etc.;
- maintaining open communication: employees can express their views and obtain information about the organization
- giving assistance: members can seek advice on personal problems as well as their work; and
- acting as a buffer between the group and management: he speaks up for his men and explains the reasons for management's decisions.

Such actions both strengthen group cohesiveness and solidarity and affirm the supervisor's leadership position in the group.

DEFINING MORALE

This brings us back to a point mentioned earlier. We had said that employee-centered supervisors contribute to high morale as well as to high production. But how can we explain units which have low morale and high productivity, or vice versa? Usually production and morale are considered separately, partly because they are measured against different criteria and partly because, in some instances, they seem to be independent of each other.

Some of this difficulty may stem from confusion over definitions of morale. Morale has been defined as, or measured by, absences from work, satisfaction with job or company, dissension among members of work groups, productivity, apathy or lack of interest, readiness to help others, and a general aura of happiness as rated by observers. Some of these criteria of morale are not subject to the influence of the supervisor, and some of them are not clearly related to productivity. Definitions like these invite findings of low morale coupled with high production.

Both productivity and morale can be influenced by environmental factors not under the control of group members or supervisors. Such things as plant layout, organizational structure and goals, lighting, ventilation, communications, and management planning may have an adverse or desirable effect.

We might resolve the dilemma by defining morale on the basis of our understanding of the supervisor as leader of a group; morale is the degree of satisfaction of group members with their leadership. In this light, the supervisor's employee-centered activities bear a clear relation to morale. His efforts to increase employee identification with the group and to strengthen his leadership lead to greater satisfaction with that leadership. By increasing group cohesiveness and by demonstrating that his influence and power can aid the group, he is able to enhance his leadership status and afford satisfaction to the group.

SUPERVISION, PRODUCTION, AND MORALE

There are factors within the organization itself which determine whether increased production is possible:

- Are production goals expressed in terms understandable to employees and are they realistic?
- Do supervisors responsible for production respect the agency mission and production goals?
- If employees do not know how to do the job well, does management provide a trainer—often the supervisor—who can teach efficient work methods?

There are other factors within the work group which determine whether increased production will be attained:

- Is leadership present which can bring about the desired level of production?
- Are production goals accepted by employees as reasonable and attainable?
- If group effort is involved, are members able to coordinate their efforts?

Research findings confirm the view that an employee-centered supervisor can achieve higher morale than a production-centered supervisor Managers may well ask what is the relationship between this and production.

Supervision is production-oriented to the extent that it focuses attention on achieving organizational goals, and plans and devises methods for attaining them; it is employee-centered to the extent that it focuses attention on employee attitudes toward those goals, and plans and works toward maintenance of employee satisfaction.

High productivity and low morale result when a supervisor plans and organizes work efficiently but cannot achieve high membership satisfaction. Low production and high morale result when a supervisor, though keeping members satisfied with his leadership, either has not gained acceptance of organizational goals or does not have the technical competence to achieve them.

The relationship between supervision, morale, and productivity is an interdependent one, with the supervisor playing an integral role due to his ability to influence productivity and morale independently of each other.

A supervisor who can plan his work well has good technical knowledge, and who can install better production methods can raise production without necessarily increasing group satisfaction. On the other hand, a supervisor who can motivate his employees and keep them satisfied with his leadership can gain high production in spite of technical difficulties and environmental obstacles.

CLIMATE AND SUPERVISION

Climate, the intangible environment of an organization made up of attitudes, beliefs, and traditions, plays a large part in morale, productivity, and supervision. Usually when we speak of climate and its relationship to morale and productivity, we talk about the merits of *democratic* versus *authoritarian* climate. Employees seem to produce more and have higher morale in a democratic climate, whereas in an authoritarian climate, the reverse seems to be true or so the researchers tell us. We would do well to determine what these terms mean to supervision.

Perhaps most of our difficulty in understanding and applying these concepts comes from our emotional reactions to the words themselves. For example, authoritarian climate is usually painted as the very blackest kind of dictatorship. This is not surprising, because we are usually expected to believe that it is invariably bad. Conversely, democratic climate is drawn to make the driven snow look impure by comparison.

Now these descriptions are most probably true when we talk about our political processes, or town meetings, or freedom of speech. However, the same labels have been used by social scientists in other contexts and have also been applied to government and business organizations, without it, it seems, any recognition that the meanings and their social values may have changed somewhat

For example, these labels were used in experiments conducted in an informal classroom setting using 11-year-old boys as subjects. The descriptive labels applied to the climate of the setting as well as the type of leadership practiced. When these labels were transferred to a management setting, it seems that many presumed that they principally meant the king of leadership rather than climate. We can see that there is a great difference between the experimental and management settings and that leadership practices for one might be inappropriate for the other.

It is doubtful that formal work organizations can be anything but authoritarian, in that goals are set by management and a hierarchy exists through which decisions and orders from the top are transmitted downward. Organizations are authoritarian by structure and need; direction and control are placed in the hands of a few in order to gain fast and efficient decision making. Now this does not mean to describe a dictatorship. It is merely the recognition of the fact that direction of organizational affairs comes from above. It should be noted that leadership in some natural groups is, in this sense, authoritarian.

Granting that formal organizations have this kind of authoritarian leadership, can there be a democratic climate? Certainly there can be, but we would want to define and delimit this term. A more realistic meaning of democratic climate in organizations is the use of permissive and participatory methods in management-employee relations. That is, a mutual exchange of information and explanation with the granting of individual freedom within certain restricted and defined limits. However, it is not our purpose to debate the merits of authoritarianism versus democracy. We recognize that within the small work group there is a need for freedom from constraint and an increase in participation in order to achieve organizational goals within the framework of the organizational movement.

Another aspect of climate is best expressed by this familiar, and true, saying: actions speak louder than words. Of particular concern to us is this effect of management climate on the behavior of supervisors, particularly in employee-centered activities.

There have been reports of disappointment with efforts to make supervisors ore employee-centered. Managers state that, since research has shown ways of improving human relations, supervisors should begin to practice these methods. Usually a training course in human relations is established; and supervisors are given this training. Managers then sit back and wait for the expected improvements, only to find that there are none.

If we wish to produce changes in the supervisor's behavior, the climate must be made appropriate and rewarding to the changed behavior. This means that top-level attitudes and behavior cannot deny or contradict the change we are attempting to effect. Basic changes in organizational behavior cannot be made with any permanence, unless we provide an environment that is receptive to the changes and rewards those persons who do change.

IMPROVING SUPERVISION

Anyone who has read this far might expect to find *A Dozen Rules for Dealing With Employees* or *29 Steps to Supervisory Success.* We will not provide such a list.

Simple rules suffer from their simplicity. They ignore the complexities of human behavior. Reliance upon rules may cause supervisors to concentrate on superficial aspects of their relations with employees. It may preclude genuine understanding.

The supervisor who relies on a list of rules tends to think of people in mechanistic terms. In a certain situation, he uses *Rule No. 3.* Employees are not treated as thinking and feeling persons, but rather as figures in a formula: Rule 3 applied to employee X = Production.

Employees usually recognize mechanical manipulation and become dissatisfied and resentful. They lose faith in, and respect for, their supervisor, and this may be reflected in lower morale and productivity.

We do not mean that supervisors must become social science experts if they wish to improve. Reports of current research indicate that there are two major parts of their job which can be strengthened through self-improvement: (1) Work planning, including technical skills, and (2) motivation of employees.

The most effective supervisors combine excellence in the administrative and technical aspects of their work with friendly and considerate personal relations with their employees.

CRITICAL PERSONAL RELATIONS

Later in this chapter we shall talk about administrative aspects of supervision, but first let us comment on *friendly and considerate personal relations*. We have discussed this subject throughout the preceding chapters, but we want to review some of the critical supervisory influences on personal relations.

Closeness of Supervision: The closeness of supervision has an important effect on productivity and morale. Mann and Dent found that supervisors of low-producing units supervise very closely, while high-producing supervisors exercise only general supervision. It was found that the low-producing supervisors:

- check on employees more frequently
- give more detailed and frequent instructions
- limit employee's freedom to do job in own way

Workers who felt less closely supervised reported that they were better satisfied with their jobs and the company. We should note that the manner or attitude of the supervisor has an important bearing on whether employees perceive supervision as being close or general.

These findings are another way of saying that supervision does not mean standing over the employee and telling him what to do and when and how to do it. The more effective supervisor tells his employees what is required, giving general instructions.

COMMUNICATION

Supervisors of high-production units consider communication as one of the most important aspects of their job. Effective communication is used by these supervisors to achieve better interpersonal relations and improved employee motivation. Low-production supervisors do not rate communications as highly important.

High-producing supervisors find that an important aid to more effective communication is listening. They are ready to listen to both personal problems or interests and questions about the work. This does not mean that they are *nosey* or meddle in their employees' personal lives, but rather that they show a willingness to listen, and do listen, if their employees wish to discuss problems.

These supervisors inform employees about forthcoming changes in work; they discuss agency policy with employees; and they make sure that each employee knows how well he is doing. What these supervisors do is use two-way communication effectively. Unless the supervisor freely imparts information, he will not receive information in return.

Attitudes and perception are frequently affected by communication or the lack of it. Research surveys reveal that many supervisors are not aware of their employees' attitudes, nor do they know what personal reactions their supervision arouses. Through frank discussion with employees, they have been surprised to discover employee beliefs about which they were ignorant. Discussion sometimes reveals that the supervisor and his employees have totally different impressions about the same event. The supervisor should be constantly on the alert for misconceptions about his words and deeds. He must remember that, although his actions are perfectly clear to himself, they may be, and frequently are, viewed differently by employees.

Failure to communicate information results in misconceptions and false assumptions. What you say and how you say it will strongly affect your employees' attitudes and perceptions. By giving them available information, you can prevent misconceptions; by discussion, you may be able to change attitudes; by questioning, you can discover what the perceptions and assumptions really are. And it need hardly be added that actions should conform very closely to words.

If we were to attempt to reduce the above discussion on communication to rules, we would have a long list which would be based on one cardinal principle: Don't make assumptions!

- Don't assume that your employees know; tell them.
- Don't assume that you know how they feel; find out.
- Don't assume that they understand; clarify.

15

20 SUPERVISORY HINTS

1. Avoid inconsistency.
2. Always give employees a chance to explain their action before taking disciplinary action. Don't allow too much time for a "cooling off" period before disciplining an employee.
3. Be specific in your criticisms.
4. Delegate responsibility wisely.
5. Do not argue or lose your temper, and avoid being impatient.
6. Promote mutual respect and be fair, impartial, and open-minded.
7. Keep in mind that asking for employees' advice and input can be helpful in decision making.
8. If you make promises, keep them.
9. Always keep the feelings, abilities, dignity and motives of your staff in mind.
10. Remain loyal to your employees' interests.
11. Never criticize employees in front of others, or treat employees like children.
12. Admit mistakes. Don't place blame on your employees, or make excuses.
13. Be reasonable in your expectations, give complete instructions, and establish well-planned goals.
14. Be knowledgeable about office details and procedures, but avoid becoming bogged down in details.
15. Avoid supervising too closely or too loosely. Employees should also view you as an approachable supervisor.
16. Remember that employees' personal problems may affect job performance, but become involved only when appropriate.
17. Work to develop workers, and to instill a feeling of cooperation while working toward mutual goals.
18. Do not overpraise or underpraise, be properly appreciative.
19. Never ask an employee to discipline someone for you.
20. A complaint, even if unjustified, should be taken seriously.

16

NOTES

DIAGNOSING THE CAUSES OF AUTOMOTIVE TROUBLES

CONTENTS

DIAGNOSING THE CAUSES OF AUTOMOTIVE TROUBLES

The number of possible difficulties encountered with an automobile is endless, and no attempt will be made to present them all. Diagnosing auto troubles requires thought and reasoning. If the principles and construction of the various parts of the care are understood, and one of the hundreds of possible troubles occurs, then simply reason it out. Determine what the trouble is, learn what might cause that trouble, and why the trouble is present. Decide whether it is in the ignition, fuel system, lubrication system, or just where it is, and then track it down by a process of elimination. Following is a list of various common troubles, each one of which is directly followed by its possible causes.

A. ENGINE TROUBLES

1. Engine fails to start
    a. Lack of gasoline - empty tank or trouble in fuel system
    b. Carburetor needs priming
    c. Poor quality of gasoline - may contain water or be old and stable
    d. Too much gasoline - cylinder may be flooded; spark plugs may be soaked; gasoline needle valve not working
    e. No pressure in fuel tank
    f. Lack of ignition current may be due to exhausted battery or broken or loose wiring
    g. Spark plugs may be sooted from over-lubrication, or the point may be burnt or corroded

2. Engine Starts But Misses
    (The missing cylinder or cylinders may be located by short circuiting each spark plug with a screwdriver. When the plug in the missing cylinder is short-circuited, no difference will be noticed in the engine. Short-circuiting a good cylinder will cause another miss and slow the engine.)
    a. Defective spark plugs
    b. Wet spark plugs, wiring or distributor
    c. Defective or dirty or wet distributor
    d. Improper or broken wiring connections
    e. Weak battery
    f. Incorrect fuel mixture
    g. Defective condenser
    h. Engine cold on a cold day
    i. Valve leakage, which might be due to
        (1) Valves adjusted too tightly
        (2) Need for grinding
        (3) Broken spring or seat
        (4) Carbon deposit

3. Engine Starts But Will Not pull
    a. Brakes dragging or hand brake set
    b. Low oil supply
    c. Defective lubrication system
    d. Water supply low, or defect in cooling system
    e. Mixture too lean or too rich

f. Leady valves or rings, causing loss of compression
g. Spark retarded or improperly timed
h. Slipping clutch
i. Trouble in the ignition system

4. Engine is Hard to Start
   a. Stiff engine due to cold weather or improper lubrication
   b. Choke not functioning properly
   c. Incorrect throttle setting
   d. Lean mixture; leaky valves; weak battery

5. Engine Overheats
   a. Water or oil supply low
   b. Defective or dirty cooling or lubrication system
   c. Spark retarded or improperly timed
   d. Mixture too rich or engine badly carbonized
   e. Too much running on low gear

6. Engine Stalls
   a. If it stops suddenly without warning, either the ignition switch was turned off accidentally or there is trouble in the ignition system.
   b. If permanent stalling is preceded by intermittent missing or stalling, look for ignition trouble.
   c. If the engine "peters out" as though through the throttle were suddenly closed all the way, look for carburetor trouble (usually dirt).
   d. If petering out is preceded by loss of power, backfiring, or missing (without muffler explosions) the trouble is most probably due to dirt in the fuel system.
   e. List of possible causes
      (1) Lack of gasoline
      (2) Dirt or water in the fuel system
      (3) Failure of fuel feed system
      (4) Defects, improper connections, dirt or water in the ignition system
      (5) Valves adjusted too tightly
      (6) Mixture too rich
      (7) Incorrect timing of valves

7. Engine Knocks
   a. Carbon knock: Most noticeable when the car climbs in a steep grade in high gear. Usually not heard when engine is warming up.
   b. Spark too far advanced: Noticeable with the throttle open and the engine pulling hard.
   c. Loose connecting-rod bearing: Heard when the engine is running idly down hill, or when it is allowed to decelerate after speeding up.
   d. Loose main bearing: Noticeable when running fast with the spark advanced
   e. Loose flywheel: Noticed when the ignition is shut off with the engine running, and then switched on when the engine has almost stopped.
   f. Loose pistons: Most noticeable when the engine is speeded up while the car is standing.
   g. Loose piston pin
   h. Lean mixture

i. Engine too hot or lacks oil
j. Valves stuck or need adjusting

8. Engine Backfires (This is always accompanied by missing.)
   a. Cold engine
   b. Spar too far retarded
   c. Fuel heating device not working
   d. Lean mixture
   e. Dirt in the carburetor
   f. Intake valve leaks, or too much clearance on exhaust valve

9. Engine Keeps Running With Switch Off
   (This is caused by overheating, which may be due to:)
   a. Ignition system - defective switch
   b. Poor oil - deposits carbon on the cylinder, and this carbon becomes red-hot, causing pre-ignition

B. STARTING MOTOR TROUBLES

1. Starting Motor Does Not Operate
   a. Battery may be weak or exhausted, or a connection may be loose
   b. Bendix drive or starting mechanism out of order
   c. Open circuit in the wiring: broken or loose wiring connections

2. Starting Motor Operates, But Not Enough to Turn Over
   a. Weak battery
   b. Engine may be unusually stiff
   c. Poor contact at battery terminals
   d. Trouble in the starting motor mechanism

C. ENGINE LUBRICATION TROUBLES

1. High Oil Consumption
   a. Leakage past pistons, or in the lubricating system
   b. Oil too light or of poor quality
   c. Pump pressure too high
   d. High engine speeds

2. Low Oil Consumption
   a. Dilution of oil by fuel
   b. Leakage of water into the oil

3. High and Low Oil Pressures

4. Oil Gauge Hand Flutters
   a. Low oil supply
   b. Leak in the piping
   c. Pump strainer dirty
   d. Intermittent clogging in the lubrication system

D. CLUTCH TROUBLES

1. Clutch Slips (Engine runs too fast in relation to car speed)
   a. Too much oil on a lubricated clutch; oil present on a dry clutch
   b. Clutch needs adjusting
   c. Weak clutch
   d. Badly worn clutch facings

2. Clutch Drags (Fails to release fully when thrown out)
   a. Adjustment too tight
   b. Rivets in the facing are protruding
   c. Clutch bearing worn or broken
   d. Clutch out of alignment

3. Clutch Spins (The drive member of the clutch fails to come to rest quickly when the clutch is thrown out)
   a. Oil on clutch brake
   b. Clutch adjusted too tightly

4. Clutch Grabs (A tendency of the clutch to take hold too suddenly)
   a. Gummed oil on clutch faces
   b. Adjustment too tight
   c. Rivets protruding from clutch facing
   d. Glazed lining

E. COOLING SYSTEM TROUBLES (Any defect in this system results in overheating the engine)

1. Not enough water in the system
2. Core passages of the radiator clogged: Cleaned by flushing with a mixture of salsoda and water
3. Faulty water in the radiator
4. Frozen water in the radiator
5. Anti-freeze in the system in hot weather
6. Leaks in the system
7. Fan belt not working properly

F. BATTERY TROUBLES

1. Defective generator or circuit breaker
2. Open circuits or poor connections
3. Low electrolyte
4. Sulphated or corroded battery terminals
5. Battery does not hold charge
   a. Car not run enough in the daytime, or not a high enough speed, for the generator to charge the battery and replace the current consumed by the lights, tarter, etc.
   b. Generator output not properly adjusted
   c. Circuit breaker not operating properly
   d. Overload on the electrical system, due to too many appliances (radio, lighters, etc.)
   e. Plates are sulphated

f. Active material of the plate grids is loose

G. CARBURETION TROUBLES

1. Mixture too rich
   a. Air cleaner dirty or clogged
   b. Improper choke adjustment
   c. Fuel pump pressure too high
   d. Nozzle oversize or improperly adjusted
   e. Leaking float, with not enough buoyancy to close the valve
   f. Float level too high; this is one of the most common causes for incorrect carburetion
   g. Leaking float valve
   h. Changing from heavy to light fuel, with the carburetor adjusted for the heavier fuel
   i. Cold intake manifold
   j. Excessive back pressure due to clogged muffler or partly clogged exhaust pipe

2. Mixture too lean
   a. Air leaks between the carburetor and the cylinders
   b. Float level set too low
   c. Fuel nozzle clogged or undersized
   d. Low pressure from fuel pump
   e. Incorrect valve timing, causing the inlet valves to close before allowing a full charge of gas into the cylinder
   f. Change from light to heavy fuel, with the carburetor adjusted to light fuel
   g. Excessively high temperatures of intake manifold or cooling system

H. REAR AXLE TROUBLES

1. Wheels do not turn
   a. Key holding the wheel may be broken
   b. Ring gear rivets sheared on differential housing
   c. Broken axle shaft, or pinion shaft coupling
   d. Broken universal joint or propeller shaft

2. Axle bucks or clashes
   a. Worn pinion shaft thrust bearing or drive gear or pinion
   b. Worn universal joint or differential pinion
   c. Broken teeth or ring gear

I. STEERING TROUBLES

1. Shimmy: Excessive vibration of the front wheels from side to side or up and down, causing a jerky motion of the steering wheel
   a. Excessive caster, or incorrect toe-in
   b. Low or unequal tire pressures
   c. Unbalanced front wheels
   d. Shock absorbers not acting properly
   e. Springs that are weak or have broken leaves
   f. Loose wheels or steering connections

2. Pulling to one side
   a. Unequal camber or caster, or one rear wheel cambered
   b. Unequal tire inflation
   c. Dragging brakes or tight wheel bearings

3. Wandering or weaving – gradual swinging of the car to one side or the other of the road
   a. Insufficient or reversed caster
   b. Excessive tightness or looseness in the steering system
   c. Unequal camber or caster
   d. Incorrect toe-in
   e. Underinflation of rear tires

4. Hard steering, especially in making turns
   a. Excessive caster or tightness in steering system
   b. Twisted axle, or improper camber
   c. Low or unequal tire inflation

J. TIRE TROUBLES

1. Tire scuffing – abrasion of the tread as it is dragged over the road surface instead of rolling on it. Caused by incorrect toe-in, or incorrect turning radius.
2. Excessive wear on one side of the tread caused by incorrect camber.
3. Several worn spots are caused by a wobbly wheel or consistently making abrupt stops.
4. Uneven wear may be caused by springs that are too flexible, allowing variations in camber, caster, or toe-in.
5. Excessive wear of the center of the tread may be due to improper alignment of the wheels or over-inflation.
6. Greater wear on the outer edges of the tread than in the center is usually due to under-inflation.

K. BRAKE TROUBLES

The most common brake trouble is slipping, which may be caused by oil, water or grease on the lining; by poor adjustment; by worn brakes linings. Sometimes the car tends to skid to one side when the brakes are applied. This means the brake on one wheel is dragging or binding, and is due to improper adjustment. Where all brakes tighten suddenly, the cause is most probably a broken near spring. Since the brakes control the safe operation of the car, they should be kept in the best possible condition. Any troubles in the brake system should be remedied immediately, and it should be kept in mind that "taking up" the brakes is sometimes a poor substitute for replacing the lining.

L. TROUBLES INDICATED BY THE EXHAUST SMOKE

1. Black and foul-smelling smoke is caused by too rich a mixture.
2. White or blue smoke means too much oil in the engine.
3. Gray smoke indicates too much fuel as well as excess oil.

www.ingramcontent.com/pod-product-compliance
Lightning Source LLC
Chambersburg PA
CBHW082206300426
44117CB00016B/2693

* 9 7 8 1 7 9 9 3 3 5 4 4 3 *